GUERRILLA
MARKETING
RESEARCH

Marketing Research Techniques
That Can Help Any Business
Make More Money

Robert J. Kaden

London and Philadelphia

Publisher's note

Every possible effort has been made to ensure that the information contained in this book is accurate at the time of going to press, and the publishers and authors cannot accept responsibility for any errors or omissions, however caused. No responsibility for loss or damage occasioned to any person acting, or refraining from action, as a result of the material in this publication can be accepted by the editor, the publisher or any of the authors.

First published in Great Britain and the United States in 2006 by Kogan Page Limited
Reprinted in 2006
Paperback edition published in 2008

120 Pentonville Road
London N1 9JN
United Kingdom
www.kogan-page.co.uk

525 South 4th Street, #241
Philadelphia PA 19147
USA

© Robert J. Kaden, 2006

The right of Robert J. Kaden to be identified as the author of this work has been asserted by him in accordance with the Copyright, Designs and Patents Act 1988.

ISBN 978 0 7494 5089 2

British Library Cataloguing-in-Publication Data

A CIP record for this book is available from the British Library.

Library of Congress Cataloging-in-Publication Data

Kaden, Robert J.
    Guerrilla marketing research : marketing research techniques that can help any business make more money / Robert J Kaden.
        p. cm.
    Includes index.
    ISBN 978-0-7494-5089-2
1. Marketing research. 2. Small business—Management. I. Title.
HF5415.2.K24 2006
658.8'3—dc22

2005033282

Typeset by Saxon Graphics Ltd, Derby
Printed and bound in the United States by Thomson-Shore, Inc.

I dedicate this book to:

Jan Muller
Joan Fox
Maryann Safely
Gil Palen
Stu Shyrer
Norm Goldring
Jay Levinson
Don Less
Ted Spiegel
Rudy Goldsmith
The hundreds of clients who have trusted my counsel over the many years
The cadre of field services and tabs firms from which I've learned the secrets of the trade
My never-to-be-forgotten family of brilliant researchers at Goldring & Company, without whose inspiration and creativity this book could not have been written
Ellie Kaden, for her everlasting support of everything I do

Contents

About the author

Bob Kaden has lived in Chicago all his life and has been married to Ellie for more years than either like to admit. He is the father of Hilary and the grandfather of Samantha. Kaden has an AA degree from Lincoln College in Lincoln, IL, and a BA in Communications from Columbia College in Chicago.

He has been in market research his entire career, spending a number of years in the research departments at various Chicago advertising agencies and, in the early 1970s, becoming President of Goldring & Company. Goldring became one of Chicago's premier research suppliers, employing a staff of more than 40 market research professionals. He and his partners sold Goldring to MAI plc, a U.K. financial and market research conglomerate, in 1989. In 1992, he started The Kaden Company and continues today to serve his market research clients.

Bob has worked extensively in the retail, banking and credit card, food, consumer package goods, health care, educational, toy, technology, and direct marketing industries. He has been involved in more than 4,000 focus group and survey studies and has pioneered many unique quantitative and qualitative market research approaches.

Over the years, he has written numerous articles on market research applications for direct marketers and lectured widely on the use of creative problem-solving techniques as they apply to research, strategic planning, and new product development processes. His speaking engagements have taken him to many U.S. cities, as well as London, Paris, and Moscow, where he addressed audiences on the use of attitude research in the direct marketing industry as well as on the application of creative problem-solving principles to marketing research problems.

For additional information contact The Kaden Company, 6677 N Lincoln Ave, Lincolnwood, IL 60712 (tel: 847–933–9400; e-mail: thekadencompany@ sbcglobal.net).

Foreword

What you don't know about research can hurt you. What you don't know can cause lost sales and missed opportunities that would hurt you to the core if you knew the details.

In this book are the details, not only of the grief that awaits you if you fail to do proper research, but also of the giddy joy you'll experience when you review your profit and loss statement and see the payoff of knowing what you're supposed to know.

A Guerrilla Marketing Attack is a 10-step process that leads you from ignorance and inactivity to action and profitability. What do you suppose is the first step of the attack? If you answered "Marketing research," you've got the momentum you'll need to succeed with your attack. Marketing without research is like groping your way across the United States. Let's hope you don't fall into the Grand Canyon.

I remember thinking that research sounded boring. The way it is treated in these pages gives it the allure and wonder of rocket science. It truly does take you into a different world – a world that exists only to those who know the ways to it. Upcoming are the ways to it.

You'll be embarking upon them for the sake of earning honest and substantial profits. Throughout your journey deeper into your customers' heads, you'll become familiar with the Guerrilla Marketing weapons of primary research, focus groups, surveys, sampling, and brainstorming.

The information that you have gleaned with your past research may answer questions that needn't have been asked. There's no sense bogging yourself down in old data when it's only current information that you seek.

You'll get that information when you see how the behemoths get theirs. You'll also realize that you can do what they do for a fraction of the cost.

Because you already have learned that not all the best things in life are free, you'll not be shocked when you learn that primary research does come at a cost.

As a Guerrilla Marketer, you know that the cost of working with outside experts is really an investment. Few investments yield returns more valuable than information that can transform your business.

With all investments, it's crucial to begin with a plan. This book helps you create a research strategy designed solely to increase the profits for your business. If it's a small business, the plan can guide you into making it a big business. Such is the power of the right kind of research.

In my Guerrilla Marketing books, I counsel small businesses to create questionnaires so as to learn more about their customers. This Guerrilla Marketing book gets down and dirty about those questionnaires.

Once you have all the information you hoped to collect, how are you supposed to organize it? How do you go about analyzing it? How can you transform its findings into profits?

In these pages are the answers to those questions along with the answers to many questions you wouldn't have thought of asking. If there are any fingerprints on the pages, blame them on Bob Kaden, who spent so many years in the deep trenches of market research that his fingers are stained green – from the profits he has mined for his clients.

The maps of centuries past do not guide successful ventures in the present. Research the way you used to do it belongs to a bygone era. Many business owners speak of taking their business to the next level.

The next level is the one you are holding in your hands. This book is your step up to it – to the quantum advance represented by *Guerrilla Marketing Research*.

Jay Conrad Levinson
Orlando, Florida

Acknowledgments

There is joy in acknowledging the people who have supported the creation of this book. To my Chicago-area research colleagues Gerry Linda of Gerry Linda Research, Nancy Weinstein of Weinstein & Associates, Howard Kirsch of StarData, and my trusted right arm Carma Park, thank you for your contributions and advice.

A big thanks goes to my Same Time Next Year men, Terry, Chuck, Nick, Larry, Jess, Albert, Hal, Dimitri, and Joe, who helped me realize I had something to say about my many years as a researcher and that undertaking this book would provide value and insight to many small and mid-sized businesses.

Thanks also to Patricia Brown, my word-processing guru. Without your help this book would probably be written in 4-point Bauhaus type.

Thanks to my mother, Thelma Cuttler, who read and reread and reread again the manuscript, saving me untold hours of editing – which I couldn't have done anyway.

And, finally, to Jay Levinson – my mentor, friend, and now my colleague. You were pivotal in helping me start my career and have been in my life ever since. For me, you have always inspired. For you, take pride and joy in the many for whom you have been an inspiration.

Introduction

Jay Conrad Levinson defines Guerrilla Marketing as "achieving conventional goals, such as profits and joy, with unconventional methods, such as investing energy instead of money." As the father of Guerrilla Marketing, he has written over 20 books on a wide variety of Guerrilla approaches.

This book takes the Guerrilla approach and applies it to marketing research. *Guerrilla Marketing Research* is therefore a practical guide for the non-professional researcher in how to conduct professional marketing research – research that can be counted upon to guide company growth. Rather than using expensive research professionals, Guerrilla Marketing Research uses personal energy and limited funds to provide the same, or even better, research results – results that will lead to greater profits.

In *Guerrilla Marketing*, Jay Conrad Levinson talks about free market research, commonly called *secondary* source research – the kind that you do at the library, on the internet, or by studying your competitors' marketing activities, or even the kind that might include a seat-of-the-pants survey. It is good to do free research and I encourage it.

But this book is not about getting research for free. It's about conducting custom-designed *primary* research the way it's done by professionals.

This book is about conducting focus groups and surveys that allow Guerrillas to know with certainty the key motivations and messages that will cause prospects to become customers and customers to buy more – *the kind of research many entrepreneurs and small and mid-sized businesses think they can't afford.*

When you finish this book, you will understand why doing primary research the right way is important to growing your business. And you will know how to get it done for far less than you might think. If that intrigues you, please buy this book.

Defining primary research

Primary market research, or information about the marketplace, can follow two general paths. One is the *customer attitude* path, which seeks to determine the attitudes and perceptions of customers and prospects. By understanding what motivates customers and prospects, marketers can develop plans for increasing their likelihood of success. This is often referred to as the *Why* of the marketplace:

- Why don't my customers spend more with me?
- Why can't I get new customers faster?
- Why isn't my advertising being more effective?

The other path is the *customer behavior* path, which seeks to determine marketplace patterns. How much money is being spent in the product categories of interest? Is the market itself growing or diminishing? Which brands and products have the strongest shares? Which television or radio programs are watched and listened to? Which magazines are read? This is referred to as the *What* of the marketplace.

And, in fact, a great deal of *What* information is free and available to the creative researcher. But this book focuses on the *Why* factor – because by clearly understanding the *Why* of your marketplace you will have a far easier time controlling the *What*.

1

Customer attitudes – should you even care?

I was looking at the results of a survey conducted for Service Merchandise, the catalog showroom company. There was a question that asked Service Merchandise customers whether purchasing from a catalog showroom was a superior, excellent, good, fair, or poor way to shop. About 25 percent said it was a superior or excellent way to shop. The remaining 75 percent, the vast majority, said it was only a good, fair, or poor way to shop. And, of these, almost one in five said it was a poor way to shop.

I was startled. I wondered how Service Merchandise's own customers could have such a low regard for shopping the Service Merchandise way.

When I presented the survey results, I asked the company management what they felt were the benefits to the customer if shopping at their catalog showrooms. The blank stares told me they weren't sure. Well, it was abundantly clear that customers weren't sure either.

I raised two other questions: Did Service Merchandise exist to serve its customers on their or its terms and what was the Service Merchandise reason for being?

Service Merchandise never really could answer those questions. It existed for about 10 years after that, mostly doing business the same way it always had. Fewer and fewer customers walked into its stores over those years.

When customers did shop, they were confronted with a slow and cumbersome shopping experience that research continued to show they hated. Service Merchandise tried running frequent sales and promotions to attract customer traffic. It put emphasis on its profitable jewelry business, basically leaving its electronics and technology business to the many new competitors that were popping up. New company management teams came and went. As the losses mounted, it tried to stay in business by closing unprofitable stores. Finally, Service Merchandise went into liquidation.

Service Merchandise was a U.S. icon. It was the first mass merchandise discount store. The original business concept was brilliant, inspired. It allowed customers to purchase at deep discounts, and all they had to do was look in a catalog to find what they wanted, fill out an order form, and wait 10 or 15 minutes while their merchandise was picked from a vast back room and put on a conveyor belt. Then all they had to do was wait for their number to be called – if there happened to be someone available calling numbers.

Of course, many times customers waited only to find that half their order was out of stock. But this wasn't so bad, at first anyway, because this was the only game in town. And they saved a lot of money for their patience.

And there is the Spiegel catalog, which during the late 70s and 80s had strong marketing management, a strong research voice, and a knack for listening intently to consumers. It's no fluke that Spiegel enjoyed their greatest success during the years marketing research was integral to making decisions.

But what Service Merchandise ultimately forgot, what Spiegel forgot, what K-Mart forgot, what Oldsmobile forgot, and what many others forget is that, *when customers become dissatisfied, you had better pay attention.* When what you are doing or what you are selling is no longer an important benefit to your customers, your days are numbered.

WHAT DOES LISTENING TO CONSUMERS REALLY MEAN?

Nothing will ever replace entrepreneurial inspiration. Those heady days when you just know your product or service will make you millions. The energy, joy, and exhausted delight that come from knowing with certainty that one day your vision will become a profitable reality.

There are legions of companies that have sprung up from the fertile minds of entrepreneurs: Leonard Lavin and Alberto-Culver; Harland Sanders and KFC; Bill Gates and Microsoft; Andrew Groove and Intel; Walt Disney and Mickey Mouse; George Halas and the Chicago Bears. And on and on. Did those geniuses listen to the customer? Probably not – at first anyway.

Market research is not intended to be a substitute for inspiration, although it can often foster breakthrough thinking. *It is intended as a connection with your customers or prospects that, if used fully, will get you where you want to go faster and more profitably.*

At the very heart of market research is the keen belief that listening to the opinions of the consumers is important. That when asked the right questions consumers will tell you what to do to make your business more profitable. That by listening to consumers you will do the smart thing far more often than if you just decide to go it alone.

Remember when Coca-Cola introduced New Coke – and failed miserably? Here is what Sergio Zyman, who was Coke's chief marketing officer at the time, had to say about listening to the consumer (*Worth Magazine*, January 2005):

> We orchestrated a huge launch [of New Coke], received abundant media coverage... were delighted with ourselves... until the sales figures started rolling in. Within weeks, we realized that we had blundered. Sales tanked, and the media turned against us. Seventy-seven days after New Coke was born, we made the second-hardest decision in company history. We pulled the plug. What went wrong? The answer was embarrassingly simple. We did not know enough about our consumers. We did not even know what motivated them to buy Coke in the first place. We fell into the trap of imagining that innovation – abandoning our existing product for a new one – would cure our ills.
>
> After the debacle, we reached out to consumers and found that they wanted more than taste when they made their purchase. Drinking Coke enabled them to tap into the Coca-Cola experience, to be part of Coke's history and to feel the continuity and stability of the brand. Instead of innovating, we should have renovated. Instead of making a product and hoping people would buy it, we should have asked customers what they wanted and given it to them. *As soon as we started listening to them,* consumers responded, increasing our sales from 9 billion to 15 billion cases a year.

In the case of New Coke, listening to the consumer might have prevented an expensive disaster. Yet as with so many businesses, large or small, there is often too much entrepreneurial ego or downright stubbornness to listen to the consumer. Particularly for small businesses, there is rarely consideration given to the importance of research and listening to the consumer. And if it is even considered, it is likely to be written off as being unaffordable.

An entrepreneur once asked, "Where would I ever get money for research? I don't even have enough money for all the boxes I should order to pack my products." He walked off and left me thinking that his new shampoo was no different from dozens of competitors and that a little research would probably have (rightly) convinced him to look for something else to sell.

One struggling restaurant owner said to me, "My customers are getting older, and I'm not attracting a young crowd. It worries me. In a couple of years many will die off. Then what?" I suggested he do a couple of focus groups with younger people in the neighborhood who hadn't visited the restaurant recently. His response was, "What will they tell me? That I should lower my prices or change my menu?"

Well, perhaps that is what they'd say. I don't really know because he was too stubborn to look at the situation objectively. Maybe they would have said that the restaurant décor was too old-fashioned or that the lighting was dim and depressing. They might have said that they remembered the food wasn't very good when they visited the restaurant umpteen years ago. Maybe they would have said something simple, like they wished the menu would offer less than the elaborate six-course dinners it featured because they always left the restaurant feeling uncomfortably stuffed.

Whatever they might have said, I assure you that the restaurant owner would have been more informed and certainly clearer about his problem.

Listening to the customer starts with listening to yourself. It means suspending your ego and setting your stubbornness aside. Ask yourself these questions the next time you're likely to go it alone:

1. If I'm wrong, how much will it cost me?
2. How long can I afford to be wrong before I run out of money?
3. Would input from customers or prospects that have no stake in whether I succeed or fail help me make better decisions?
4. Do I know with certainty why prospects go to a competitor rather than me?
5. Have I asked customers and prospects what they need and want from me and my business?
6. Do I know if my customers think I'm giving them what they need and want?
7. Do I know what else I can provide customers so that they'll pay me more – and be happier about it?
8. Do customers and prospects know the benefits of buying from me?
9. Do I feel that I can't afford market research?
10. Can I accept the possibility that my customers might be smarter than I am in helping my business grow?

DO CUSTOMERS REALLY TELL YOU THE TRUTH?

It never really made sense to me, but I have encountered many business types who don't use research because they think customers will lie to them. Or that customers and prospects will be unjustly critical. In my 35 years in market research conducting over 4,000 focus groups and 1,500 surveys, I have never run into a respondent in a focus group or analyzed data from a survey where it was evident that customers or prospects were lying or were overly critical just out of spite.

No, customers don't lie. *They don't really know how to lie about your business because they haven't a clue what you want to hear.* Mostly, they don't care enough about your business to tell you anything other than the truth – other than what comes to their minds at the moment you ask them a question.

A bigger problem is that you often get customers or prospects who don't think very deeply about the issues that you are researching. Therefore, the real challenge in talking with customers is in getting them to give you enough depth of thought so that their answers mean something that allows you to take actions that result in greater sales. It is never an issue of lying. It is always the issue of getting to the real truth!

Note the following give and take from an actual focus group for a home improvement retailer:

Moderator question: What is the most important thing that will cause you to come into our stores more often?

Consumer answer: Lower your prices.

MQ: Besides lowering prices, what would be important?

CA: Probably faster checkout. There are usually long lines when I go to any of your stores.

MQ: Anything else?

CA: Well, it would be nice if the employees knew more about the products. Usually, they can't answer my questions. I think I know more about the products than the people working at your stores.

Look back at the line of questioning. The moderator asked the initial question in a totally objective manner. Stopping there, without further moderator probing, the indicated action would have been to lower prices. I will also tell you that there is not a marketing problem in the world to which customers won't first respond, "I'll buy more from you if you cut the prices." And it's always a red herring. It's not a lie. It's a knee-jerk customer response – and, while it's a legitimate response, it can't be taken at face value.

It is always your job as the researcher to dig below the surface – to probe customers again and again to uncover the below-the-surface factors that will motivate them to buy more. Think of an onion with its many layers. It's the same with customers. They don't lie. They give you what's top-of-mind, and you have to be smart enough to know what to accept and act upon and what to discard.

In this example, chances are that the customers would be as likely to buy more from the home improvement retailer if they knew they could get in and out of the store faster. Or that they might be inclined to visit the store more often if employees were more knowledgeable.

Customers don't tell us what we do or don't want to hear. They simply respond to our questions. The tale of an insightful research study, then, is in asking the right questions in the right manner. Chapter 9 on focus groups goes into detail on how to probe customer motivations effectively.

Certainly there are times when lowering prices is, in fact, the right answer, or perhaps the only answer. But the street is lined with failed marketing programs and obscure products for which marketers took customers and prospects literally and simply lowered prices to compete. Usually it is more an issue of providing better value than providing better prices.

As you use research, you will begin to understand those factors that will make a big difference. Sometimes when you've tried all the rest, when you've probed deeply and there is nothing left to make you competitive, price becomes your only point of leverage. But following a price strategy can be perilous, as has become evident in the airline industry.

The inability of American, United, Delta, and USAir to differentiate themselves on aspects of value has brought them to the brink. Not a single carrier has been able to convince flyers that paying a little more to fly them is worth it. As a result they continue to compete on price alone and seem to be in a never-ending financial spiral – downward. Someday one of them might figure out how to add enough value to justify raising prices.

WILL I REALLY LEARN ANYTHING I DON'T ALREADY KNOW?

In countless research presentations, I've heard clients say, "You aren't telling me anything I don't already know." I always found this a defensive and self-defeating attitude. It smacks of someone who is unsure or lacks discipline to follow his or her own convictions. If it's something you already know, I've reasoned, why aren't you doing it?

If research tells you what you think you know, but haven't acted upon – great! Act upon it. If it confirms what you've already been doing – great. Continue doing it, and learn how to do it better.

Gerry Linda of Gerald Linda and Associates Marketing says:

> Sometimes research will confirm your pet theory about customers, the market, the competition, your product's advantages and disadvantages. If this is the case, have you wasted your money? Absolutely not! Turning a theory into a fact is a highly useful outcome. It allows you to move forward with confidence. And you're likely to spot a nuance in the data that will help you move ahead better.

The point is simple. Customers and prospects are the ultimate judges of your success. If you listen to them closely, you'll hear many ideas for growing your business. While you can always decide not to follow their advice, failure to listen is a much bigger mistake.

DOES RESEARCH WORK FOR ALL TYPES OF BUSINESSES?

Research works as long as you have customers, prospects, or both. Research works everywhere, for any business, and for any product or service for which people can give you opinions. It may even mean doing research among your own employees.

Research will help any business determine the potential for making more money, whether that business happens to be selling gaskets to other manufacturers or cereal to children. Some of my more interesting clients include:

- a manufacturer selling switching equipment to phone companies;
- a cemetery selling grave sites;
- a company selling wallpaper over the internet;

- a catalog selling office furniture;
- a company selling pantyhose to women who weigh more than 250 pounds;
- a company trying to convince smokers to quit;
- a tobacco company trying to convince men who chew to change brands of chewing tobacco;
- a mail order music club trying to convince members to buy DVDs;
- a technology company trying to convince web developers to use its software;
- a popcorn company interested in creating a new popcorn flavor;
- a museum generating donations;
- a charity needing to increase donations;
- a publisher of encyclopedias selling its yearly updates;
- a publisher of art selling its limited-edition prints;
- a health insurance carrier trying to get policy holders to participate in its wellness program.

2

Asking the right questions

Don't take it lightly. Asking the right questions takes thought. It's not as easy as it first appears. But determining the right questions is important in realizing clear and concise research objectives. Always begin by asking yourself, "What is the most important question I want answered, what is the second most important, third most, etc.?"

Without clear research questions, it's impossible to determine whether the answers you get will be meaningful. Without clear questions, you will get answers that are likely to suggest actions you are unwilling or unable to take.

Think about the company that sells wallpaper by phone or on the internet and follow this conversation:

Company marketing director: Something must be wrong with my catalog because a lot of people who look through it don't buy.

Researcher: What people?

CMD: A lot of people request a catalog from the company and then don't buy when it's mailed to them.

Researcher: What makes you think it has anything to do with your catalog?

CMD: Well, they asked for one, didn't they? Why would they ask for one if they weren't interested in buying?

Researcher: Maybe they were just shopping around and still might buy in the future? Maybe they love the catalog. Maybe the reasons they didn't buy have more to do with things other than the catalog.

CMD: What do you suggest?

Researcher: I would suggest studying why people don't buy and the role of the catalog in the buying process.

If the marketing director's initial statement ("Something must be wrong with my catalog because a lot of people who look through it don't buy") was accepted on face value, the research would be very narrow in its scope. Further, the results might suggest the need for a great many expensive changes to the catalog that, if followed, might make the catalog better but still not influence the number of people who buy from it.

By studying the larger question ("What is the role of the catalog in the buying process?"), a much greater opportunity exists for learning the problems of converting catalog requesters to buyers and whether changes to the catalog would be a major or minor influence to this conversion.

Here's another example from the president of a company selling gifts:

President: I want research to convince my biggest customer [a large retailer] to carry more of my Christmas gift line.

Researcher: What if the research shows people don't like your line?

President: Well, I know the products in my line sell better than my competitor's lines. So somebody must like my stuff.

Researcher: What products in your line sell better?

President: The products we put in designer boxes really sell well.

Researcher: Maybe it has more to do with the design of your boxes than with the products themselves. Maybe we should be testing your package designs against your competitor's package designs?

President: I know most people want a great gift box that they can just put under the tree without having to wrap it. But doesn't the product inside have something to do with it?

Researcher: I think we have two issues to research. First, we should determine the strongest graphic designs for your boxes compared to your competitor's. Then, we should determine which products work best with your strongest boxes.

President: Right. That way we can convince them that our box designs are better and should get more display space, and that the products we put in our boxes are the most appropriate for the box design itself.

It's easy for research to provide answers to questions. It is hard to determine whether the questions are worth answering in the first place. When creating questions for research, it is usually prudent to get input from others. Follow these guidelines:

1. Write down all the questions that you have for the research.
2. Rewrite the same questions but use different wording. If rewriting gives you a different slant on them, create a new question list.
3. Read each question one at a time to an associate. Pose this question to your associate: "What will be learned if we get answers to this question?"
4. If you find that your associate's response doesn't reinforce what you hope to learn from the question, your question is unclear. Reword it again.
5. Have the associate take your questions and conduct the same exercise with yet a third associate. Again, reword as necessary.

You will be amazed at how this simple process will make your questions more succinct and expressive of what you want to learn. And, as a result, your research will become even more targeted and action-oriented.

WHERE ARE YOUR GREATEST OPPORTUNITIES FOR MAKING MORE MONEY?

There are many ways to make more money. They include:

- Get more customers into your door.
- Get current customers to spend more each time they buy.
- Get current customers to buy more often so that they don't go elsewhere to buy products that they would be just as likely to buy from you.
- Improve product lines.
- Add product lines.

- Negotiate lower prices from vendors but keep current prices to customers.
- Cut overhead.
- Motivate employees to sell more.
- Grow the market for the products you sell.
- Increase or change the number of channels by which you offer your products, making it less expensive to distribute your products.

When thinking about your research questions, think about implementing the results of the research. If you learned that you have to add new products to grow your business, is this viable for you? If you have to spend money to grow your market, can you make an investment that would pay off? You should continually be asking yourself, "Once I get the answers to my research questions will it be realistic for me to implement the research results?"

In going through this process, many times the typical answer I have received from clients is, "I don't know what I'd do until I see the results of the research." While this can be a fair answer, it also smacks of research that might be interesting, but results never acted upon.

Getting answers to interesting questions where taking action is out of the question can be a monumental waste of time and money. But answering questions where actions can be taken, if indicated, are always worth the effort.

Take the research for the wallpaper company again. Say the results suggest that the real reason people don't buy when they get the catalog is because they are afraid to buy wallpaper sight unseen using only a catalog or the internet as their guide. What actions might the company take if this proves to be the major stumbling block?

Maybe they should open retail stores so that customers can see their products before they buy – an unlikely solution. Maybe they should offer free returns if the customer doesn't like the wallpaper once they see it – a reasonable but perhaps profit-sapping solution. Maybe they should more strongly educate potential buyers that their policy is to send them free samples of wallpaper prior to purchase if the customer so requests, which would be easy and perhaps cost-effective. Maybe the company can't afford to do anything that is cost-effective that would address this problem. But I would doubt that as well.

While there is no apparent solution to this dilemma, it highlights why many research studies are not action-oriented. If you were Kraft or General Foods, that might not be such a problem. The cost of such research is often an insignificant part of their profits.

But for a small company, the cost of research can divert funds that could be used for other important initiatives. Therefore, it is far more important that those new to research be able to conceptualize solutions or areas where action might be taken prior to engaging in research. Anticipating possible actions that you might take would make you far more likely to conduct research that could lead to a profitable outcome.

UNDERSTANDING THE NEEDS OF YOUR CUSTOMER

Consumers buy products because they *need* them, e.g., a car to go back and forth. They buy products because they *want* them, e.g., a BMW because it makes a strong statement about their success. They buy products they *wish* for, e.g., a Porsche because it is a symbol of automobile perfection. They buy products they *desire*, e.g., a PT Cruiser because it takes them back to their childhood.

Needs, wants, wishes, and desires. They are all part and parcel of why people buy. And they are all critical to understanding how to keep your current customers and attract new ones.

Recently, I found myself choosing a new dry cleaner when I *wanted* same-day service and my old cleaner couldn't accommodate me. This situation was beyond my simple *need* for clean clothes.

I *wished* every time I went into the restaurant closest to my house that they would put families with little kids who are likely to whine in one dining room and reserved another room for adult peace and quiet. I finally found one in my neighborhood that did just that, and have enjoyed more than two dozen dinners there in the last year.

And, although I have no real need, want or wish to spend $2 a day on coffee, I certainly *desire* my daily Starbucks Grande.

With products such as perfume, liquor, automobiles, and choice of an airline or hotel, it is essential to understand the *wishes and desires* of customers rather than their largely fulfilled *needs and wants*. Even with products such as cereals, instant dinners, or computers, there may be many needs and wants still unfulfilled, but wishes and desires also play a pivotal role in the choices we make.

We are in an ever-increasing and competitive economy. *For most products and services, we have choices that are far beyond the simple fulfillment of basic needs*. We have moved to a point where uncovering and exploiting what might have been a significant need or want several years ago is now basic to just being competitive.

In an article entitled "How can we help you: the costly challenge of discovering consumers' unmet needs – and meeting them," published in the *Wall Street Journal* (New York), January 2005 (Classroom edition), D. Ball, S. Ellison, and J. Adamy said:

> companies are digging deeper into shoppers' homes... to discover "unmet needs" and then design new products to meet them...
>
> P&G appears to have hit the jackpot with an unmet need it discovered among those consumers who wash their own cars. They told P&G that half of the time they devoted to washing the car was actually spent drying the car, so that water spots won't form. For these consumers, P&G designed Mr. Clean AutoDry Carwash, a sponge along with a nozzle and a liquid-soap cartridge that attaches to a garden hose. A filter in the nozzle removes the minerals in water that cause the spots...
>
> The AutoDry product is on track to generate more than $100 million in first-year sales.

Good research digs below the obvious. While it should tell you if you are doing the basic job in meeting your customer's basic needs, that is often not enough. *Good research should strip away the apparent in an effort to surface exploitable advantages.* It should determine the unmet wants, wishes, and desires that, if you addressed them, will motivate customers and prospects to choose you rather than one of the many competitive options that they constantly face.

PUTTING RESEARCH QUESTIONS INTO RESEARCH OBJECTIVES

In order to uncover unmet wants, needs, and desires, you have to ask the right questions. Those new to research usually want questions answered that are so broad they are impossible for research to address economically. Therefore, it is imperative that research *questions* are clearly and concisely translated to research *objectives*.

A client that sells Easter gifts in retail stores said to me, "I think I can sell my line of gifts at higher prices, but I have to prove that people will spend more. My question is, 'Can I do research to prove that the higher-priced line will sell?'" Given this question, we set about defining exact research objectives.

The following overall objective was developed: "In planning for the coming Easter season, Acme is developing new ideas for its line of Easter gifts. The new gifts come in packages that are a strong departure from previous lines. The product line sells at $5 per gift. Additionally, Acme has conceptualized themed gifts at a higher $10 price point and wishes to determine how they would sell in comparison to its lower-priced line."

Secondary objectives for this research are to understand:

- The unit and dollar share of business Acme might expect from its line of $5 and $10 Easter gifts as compared to its previous line and to lines of competitive Easter gifts.
- The price points that generate the greatest interest. What is the price sensitivity to Acme gifts priced at $5 and $10 versus competitive gifts priced the same way?
- How are the Acme gifts priced at $5 and $10 perceived in comparison to competitive gifts in terms of being:
  - gifts of good value;
  - gifts that feature good toy / candy quality;
  - gifts that have good play value;
  - gifts that are colorful and pleasing to look at.
- How does the current Acme gift line featuring unique packaging compare to gifts packaged in the past? Does the new packaging have the same gift-giving potential as baskets or tins?

With these objectives agreed upon, it became easy to write a questionnaire that addressed them.

The art of digging from a general question to a clear research objective takes some work. Redefinition or stating the problem differently is another technique for digging below the obvious. Just as you reworded your research questions to ensure clarity, generating precise research objectives is also important.

The following is another illustration of how digging below the obvious will generate more clearly defined objectives:

1. Write down your research objective, for example "The overall objective of the research is to determine how to get customers to buy from me more often."
2. State the objective a second way, for example "The overall objective of the research is to determine whether better customer service will cause customers to buy from me more often."
3. State the objective yet a third way, for example "The overall objective of the research is to determine whether offering customers incentives would get them to buy from me more often."

Suppose #2 is determined to be the most important research objective. You would then create secondary research objectives that further elaborate on the overall objective. In this case, it would be to determine whether better customer service will cause customers to buy more often. A secondary research objective might be: "To determine how customers rate the customer service in the following areas: being knowledgeable; being friendly; providing answers quickly; being able to understand my problems; offering solutions that I hadn't considered; etc."

However, if #3 is determined to be your most important research objective, the secondary research objectives then might become: "Determine the incentives that might be offered to customers that would cause them to buy more often, for example: What incentives do other companies offer that cause customers to be loyal? Could a customer loyalty program that provides discounts for frequent purchases be effective? What levels of discount would be adequate? Could awarding points that could be redeemed for merchandise, travel, etc. be effective?"

DEFINING RESEARCH OBJECTIVES FURTHER

The further you redefine your research objectives, the more likely the information that you collect will be richer and action-oriented.

Another effective technique for determining precise research objectives is to conduct three to five in-depth interviews with some of your customers. You'll be amazed at the feedback your own customers will provide you if only you ask.

Conduct these interviews in person or over the phone, but in a very businesslike manner. This is not about being a friend to your customers and hoping they'll be nice to you in return. It is about being able to get their honest, objective feedback. And, because you don't want them to feel defensive or on the spot, you might try opening the conversation as follows:

> Hello, John. We're going to undertake some research among our customers and we're trying to formulate the objectives. Would you be willing to give me your objective feedback on some questions I'm thinking about? Good!

1. Sometimes customers come to us because the places they usually buy from are out of stock. If you were me, what would you say that would encourage them to buy more from me, not just when my competitor is out of stock?

2. If you knew that a customer was buying from me 50 percent of the time, what would you suggest that would cause the customer to increase that buying to 75 percent?

3. Sometimes I hear that our customer service is great and sometimes not so great. What is it about customer service in our industry that you like and don't like?

Certainly, these interviews can take a different tack, given your relationship with the customer and your research questions. The point is to try to keep it objective and not to be defensive. Listen to your customer and read between the lines. You'll find that your research objectives will sizzle with clarity.

Customer feedback is important not only in *evaluating* your products and performance, but in *determining areas* that should be evaluated in the first place.

WHAT ACTIONS MIGHT YOU TAKE?

Being clear on the actions that you might take is far more important for smaller companies than it is for larger ones. Large companies often conduct what is referred to as *exploratory* research. This is research for which no particular problems need solving. Large companies often conduct exploratory research because they know that it is important to stay ahead of consumer thinking and to spot trends as they are beginning. They also hope to get an inkling of unmet needs, wants, wishes, or desires the consumer might express and that they could be the first to exploit.

When planning a project, a research director at a large food company said, "We don't really have any idea what we might learn from your focus groups, but if something is changing out there we have to know." Conventional thinking in large companies is that, if they don't discover it first, a competitor will. Exploratory research is a first line of defense.

For Guerrillas, the cost associated with conducting exploratory research without first thinking through how the research will be used is usually unwise – and costly. When looking at the results, internal arguments often surface as to what actions, if any, the research might be suggesting. Often, a feeling starts to pervade the company that research doesn't really lead to anything other than conjecture and supposition.

Therefore, define several actions that you might take if the research points more to doing A than doing B, or if it suggests that C is the best way to go even though you know that you can't afford to do C.

DEFINING YOUR ACTIONS

At this point you will have clearly defined research objectives. Now you can begin to determine the actions that you'd likely take when the results come in. The following format can be useful for brainstorming potential actions:

1. State the overall objective that you would like answered by the research.

2. State the secondary objective that you would like answered by the research.

3. Write down what you think the findings of the research could be, that is, what you could learn.
   a. I might learn that _____.
   b. I might learn that _____.
   c. Continue until all options are written down.
4. Write down what actions you would consider taking on the basis of your learning:
   For 3a. Action #1 _____ Action #2 _____ Action #3 _____.
   For 3b. Continue until at least three actions for all findings are identified.

In completing this exercise, it is important to ask yourself whether you have the people, the resources, or the money to take the actions that you contemplate. If so, you have created action-orientated research scenarios. If not, you should rethink both your research objectives and actions steps.

EXPLORATORY RESEARCH

As previously discussed, exploratory research is research that is conducted even though the marketer isn't sure it will result in any particular action. Such research is regarding as a fishing expedition, in that research objectives can be broad, vague, and ill defined. Nevertheless, exploratory research allows marketers to keep up with ever-changing market conditions and may tip them off as to areas where a well-defined research project is needed.

I am not against exploratory research for small companies, if your budget allows. Conducting research that suggests actions that you might be unwilling or unable to take can, indeed, be helpful. Research outcomes that indicate an action that you are unable to take can open your eyes to the realities of the marketplace. Even if you can't do anything about them, they can force you to rethink your priorities and perhaps put limited resources to use where they will do the most good.

Further, exploratory research may save money by steering you away from areas where your resources would produce only a limited impact. It could be a waste, for example, to venture forward in areas where you are likely to have little impact. In fact, I would say fully half the exploratory research studies I've conducted point to action steps where the client fails to act because the expenditures necessary to address the findings adequately are not affordable.

Exploratory research findings that prove arduous for you to implement may actually give you a head start counteracting potential threats that will eventually come from a competitor with deeper pockets.

3

How the big guys do it – large-company research

I have strong opinions about large-company research. On one hand, I have great admiration for large-company researchers who strive mightily to have their voices heard and to make a difference. At best, they are the voice of the consumer, and they are listened to and respected for the clear direction that they provide their companies.

On the other hand, I find great frustration in the second-class status that research departments occupy at many large companies. At the worst, they are the reluctant, silent keepers of information. They are unable to navigate the many levels of company management in order to communicate research findings to the people who are willing and able to take action. They are unable to sell the value of what they do and too meek to fight the corporate fight necessary to ensure that the research they conduct is used to its fullest.

Certainly, this criticism could describe many departments in a large company. But it seems particularly attributable to the research function. In the almost 100 large companies that I have served, I have not known one researcher who became the CEO or COO or even ascended to the board of directors. Usually such status goes to people who have toiled in finance, operations, or marketing and have been successful in getting the attention and trust of top management.

In 2003, 34,000 new products were launched – and 90 percent failed. Jack Trout at Trout & Partners states that the average U.S. family turns to the same 150 items for as much as 85 percent of its household needs –

exhibiting a strong disdain for most of the new products that marketers throw at it.

The irony is that effectively communicated good research can prevent much of this unnecessary waste of money and effort. But this will only happen when management in large companies begin to listen more intently to research people and when research people become more effective in getting them to listen. Hopefully, this is not an issue for you and your company.

In any event, large companies, or any companies for that matter, have only two general categories of research to choose from. Their studies are either strategic or tactical in nature.

STRATEGIC VERSUS TACTICAL RESEARCH

There is a saying that, "if you don't know your destination, no road will get you there." This is certainly true of achieving success in the marketplace. If you don't know what you want to accomplish, how will you ever know if you have accomplished it?

There are two kinds of research that large companies undertake: 1) *strategic research*, which helps to determine the most promising and profitable courses of action; and 2) *tactical research*, which helps to determine how best to achieve the course of action deemed to be most promising.

Strategic research studies seek to determine:

- the needs, wants, wishes, and desires in the marketplace and how customers and prospects are being served by companies hoping to capture their loyalty;
- the likely demographic targets for the products or services being sold (e.g., older or younger customers, big or small families, higher- or lower-income families, etc.);
- the likely psychographic targets for the products and services (e.g., early adopters, reluctant followers, technology averse, etc.);
- the strength and weakness of the companies or brands in the marketplace as measured by how they are perceived by the targets (e.g., company image or brand image);
- the gaps in the marketplace or the areas in which companies or brands fail to deliver what is desired by customers and prospects (e.g., the opportunities that exist for strengthening your hold on the market and/or for exploiting competitive weaknesses);
- new product opportunities that exist.

Strategic research is about creating a road map and deciding the best direction to drive. Tactical research is about determining the best roads for getting to the final destination.

Tactical research studies seek to reinforce your strategic direction by determining:

- whether the benefits delivered by your products or services are in keeping with your strategic direction;
- the improvements or changes that should be made to your products and services so that your strategic direction is strengthened;
- the improvements or changes that should be made to the manner in which you serve your customers so that your strategic direction is strengthened;
- the most convincing messages for communicating your strategic direction;
- the most compelling executions when advertising or promoting your products or services;
- the strongest packaging for your products that reinforces your strategic direction;
- the strongest name for your products or services that reinforces your strategic direction;
- how well your communication efforts are being seen, heard, remembered, and acted upon;
- which new ideas, products, or services are worth pursuing that will strengthen your strategic direction.

Tactical research is about ensuring that all the important details essential to achieving your strategic direction are effectively executed.

SETTING RESEARCH PRIORITIES

Large companies often conduct both strategic and tactical research studies at the same time. For them, there are always large road map issues to contemplate, and advertising, packaging, pricing, product, or other smaller tactical issues to explore.

As such, the cycle of research studies becomes hazy. Studies designed to provide strategic direction often surface meaningful tactical changes, while tactical studies may suggest an alternative or modified strategic direction.

Practically speaking, most large consumer-goods companies will budget for at least one large strategic study per year. And, often, one study might encompass several brands and product categories. Further, mega-companies like Kraft and General Foods may budget for dozens of strategic studies across a myriad of business units.

Large banks, such as Bank One or Citibank, or retailers such as Home Depot, Staples, or Best Buy, may conduct an overriding strategic study somewhat less often. They are not as prone to new competition that suddenly pops up or to drastically changing trends. As such, they are less likely to shift their strategic direction as often as companies selling consumer products. Nevertheless, they will always be questioning their strategies and exploring opportunities that can be addressed by less ambitious tactical research.

There tends to be little rhyme or reason in the way tactical studies are planned. Some companies will follow firm schedules for when various issues are to be studied throughout the year. Additionally, many tactical questions will surface and unplanned research will be undertaken at a moment's notice.

Other companies will simply conduct studies as issues arise. There may be a question about changing the advertising approaches. R&D might decide it needs funds for testing new products or for assessing improvements to current products. Logos, packaging graphics, line-extension opportunities, and other such questions might take center stage where research is indicated.

Essentially, it is less important for large companies to set strict priorities than it is for them to establish research as an important contributor to their decision making. Studies usually get done when they are needed and will have impact. That is usually priority enough.

WHAT KINDS OF STUDIES DO LARGE COMPANIES CONDUCT?

There are two types of market research studies: *qualitative* studies and *quantitative* studies.

Qualitative studies

Results from qualitative studies are not indicative of the opinions held by a larger population. They are not projectable to the attitudes held by customers or prospects as a whole.

Results from qualitative studies are best used to clarify objectives, to provide background information, or as thought starters, hypotheses producers, or indicators of what might work for customers or prospects at large. Qualitative research studies consist of a small sampling of the population and include:

- *Focus groups* – Generally a two-hour discussion revolving around questions and issues deemed important and consisting of a moderator and 8 to 10 respondents.
- *Mini focus groups* – A one- to two-hour discussion consisting of a moderator and four to six respondents covering the same topics as a full focus group. Mini focus groups are a less expensive option to larger focus groups.
- *Dyads and triads* – Most likely a one-hour discussion consisting of a moderator and two or three respondents. Issues discussed tend to be more limited in nature than in focus or mini focus groups.
- *In-depth personal interviews* – Generally a 30- to 60-minute give and take between a moderator and one respondent. Personal interviews are used when the topic might be sensitive and difficult to discuss in a group setting and also when it is important to obtain respondent attitudes without the influence of other respondents.
- *Observation studies* – Usually consist of a researcher observing respondents as they go about tasks related to the marketer's products. These studies might include placing a video camera in a respondent's home or place of work, for example, to record his or her movements and actual behavior under normal conditions. Researchers have learned that respondents often say one thing in focus groups but behave differently. This is because they can be quite unaware of why they behave as they do. As a result, observation studies have become more popular in recent years as a means of better understanding the consumer.
- *Brainstorming and other idea-generation processes* – Brainstorming and other idea-generation processes can take place in any configuration of the qualitative approaches discussed, but their aim is to generate new ideas, not to discuss customer or prospect issues and motivations. In Chapter 10 there is a discussion of brainstorming and ideation processes.

Quantitative studies

Results from quantitative studies are indicative of what is true for the population as a whole. While qualitative studies help determine the issues to study, quantitative studies determine which of those issues are important.

Quantitative studies consist of larger and projectable samplings of the population and include:

- *Segmentation studies* – The backbone studies that help set the strategic direction for large companies. They determine the demographics and attitudes that customers and prospects have when making purchase decisions in the category being studied. They also measure attitudes or images held about the various companies, brands, or products that compete. Segmentation studies are expensive and often include sophisticated statistical procedures for determining the various market segments that exist. But they are extremely important in understanding which appeals will be most effective to various segments of the market and to winning them over. Segmentation studies are also referred to as image and attitude studies, psychographic/typographic studies, or simply background studies.
- *Communication studies* – After the strategic direction for a company, brand, or product is set, developing communication goals is often the next step. That is, various approaches communicating the strategic direction are developed and explored. Communication studies determine which approach is most compelling and believable and should become the communication "strategy" or communication "cornerstone" for motivating customers and prospects to buy.
- *Advertising execution studies* – A clear communication strategy will serve as the guiding principle for developing various advertising approaches. Advertising execution studies determine which commercials or print ads most strongly communicate the strategy and are likely to capture the customer's attention. Ad execution studies ensure that the message being communicated is, in fact, being communicated as intended.
- *Advertising awareness and tracking studies* – Advertising awareness studies are designed to measure brand awareness, advertising awareness, and recall of the advertising content that exists in the minds of customers and prospects. Most often, they also include measurement of attitudes or images held toward the various companies, brands, or products that compete in the marketplace. Ad tracking studies are usually undertaken yearly, although they often are done more frequently. If the goal is to track changes that might have occurred in awareness or attitudes in the previous 12 months, a yearly study is enough. If the goal is to observe changes in awareness that might occur during the year, quarterly or even monthly tracking studies are undertaken.
- *Name studies* – Large companies usually consider a number of names for a new product or service that they are introducing. Name studies

determine which name is most compelling for generating trial of the brand, and for determining whether it is enhancing the strategic direction and the communication goals that the company has set.

- *Packaging studies* – As with name studies, large companies will consider any number of packaging approaches for a product. They will consider various package sizes, configurations, and graphics. Packaging studies will determine which package alternative stands out and whether it supports the communication goals of the brand.
- *Price studies* – Price studies help determine the optimum price that can be charged for products before demand suffers. They can also help determine if lower demand at a higher price could end up producing greater profits.
- *Screening studies* – Large companies are often faced with a variety of options when it comes to improving current products or introducing new products. They might be considering dozens of new line extensions or formulation changes for current products. They could have literally hundreds of new products or services under consideration, or a multitude of packaging improvements or product name changes could be under consideration. Screening studies determine the alternatives that hold the greatest promise.
- *Product testing* – Product development is always being undertaken at large companies. A new product might be developed to address an unmet need or improvements developed for current products. Product testing will determine if introducing a new product is indicated or if improving a current product will result in a competitive advantage.

TEST MARKET RESEARCH

The cost of marketing a new product can easily top $50 million. Changing the image of an existing company, brand, or product in the mind of consumers can be equally expensive. No matter how many market research studies might have been conducted indicating potential success, nothing can simulate the real conditions in the marketplace.

For example, McDonald's research on pizza indicated that they could produce a product people liked. But when they test-marketed it in a limited number of restaurants and markets, they discovered that it did not generate the sales necessary to roll it out to the entire system.

The same is true for many large companies such as Kraft or General Mills. They certainly have conducted research studies for a plethora of new products that suggested success was just around the corner. Test marketing often proved otherwise.

Many of the same types of research studies previously outlined will be conducted in test markets. But given actual market conditions, the frequency with which customers actually purchase products can be far more accurately gauged, as can the many other elements that go together in making a product successful.

DEVELOPING NEW PRODUCTS

Large companies are continually using research to conceptualize new ideas. Teams of marketing, product development, and R&D people strive mightily to find the next multimillion-dollar blockbuster product.

New products are the life blood of large companies. It's a truism that, if they're not one step ahead of the competition in uncovering and exploiting unmet needs, wants, wishes, or desires in the marketplace, they'll fall behind a worthy competitor before they know it.

Take any of these recently introduced new products:

- Febreze Scentstories – a P&G-developed air freshener that looks like a CD player and automatically gives off a new and different scent every 30 minutes. This product addresses a consumer complaint that after 30 minutes they adjust to the scent and can't smell it anymore.
- C2 – Coca-Cola's reduced-calorie, reduced-carbohydrate cola. It was, at the time, their biggest new-product introduction since Diet Coke.
- Pfizer's new Listerine Pocket Paks – thin, edible, plastic-like mouthwash strips that generated $175 million in sales in their first year.

All these products can be easily duplicated. But the very fact that a company is the first to introduce a new product provides it with a strong head start and the enviable position of being the market leader.

There are many other types of market research studies that large companies undertake. Sophisticated studies such as market share predictive modeling, conjoint analysis, and discrete choice analysis are but a few that large companies will often use. These are briefly discussed in Chapter 16 on statistical techniques.

But Guerrillas would be well served by sticking to the more basic research approaches that have been listed and that are discussed throughout this book. The more advanced techniques are best saved for a time when the research essentials have been mastered.

4

How to get started

UNDERSTANDING CURRENT OR POTENTIAL OPPORTUNITIES

Research can be about a number of general goals:

1. understanding what will make customers who do purchase the kinds of products or services you sell spend more with you than they do with your competitors;
2. understanding what will make consumers who purchase the kinds of products or services you sell buy them more often from you than from your competitors;
3. understanding what will make consumers who don't buy the kinds of products and services you sell begin buying them – and buy them from you rather than your competition;
4. determining if manufacturing your products less expensively will not negatively affect your sales and therefore will increase your profits;
5. determining if you can raise prices on your products or services and not negatively affect sales or profits.

Outside of purely academic curiosity, I can't think of any other reason whatsoever that you'd want to spend money on research. *If you aren't trying to attract your competitors' customers, convince your customers to buy more often from you, increase the size of the market itself, or increase profits by cutting cost or raising prices, you don't need market research.*

There are thousands of questions that you can ask your customers – or your competitors' customers – but there is only one reason to ask them. And that reason is to give you the best direction to make the most money possible. The trick, of course, is in determining which of the above five areas offers you the greatest potential and then asking the right questions to produce that advantage.

KNOWING WHAT QUESTIONS TO ASK

Often findings from research fail to result in clearly defined opportunities. This is usually because the right questions weren't asked in the first place. In such instances, the information generated did little more than point to the questions that you should have really been asking.

This is not necessarily bad and may even be unavoidable. The best-planned research will generate answers but will almost always beget new questions. The operative word in research is "search." Coming up short in one search can pinpoint where to start the next.

That is to say, getting answers is simple. Asking the right questions in the first place can be difficult. Archimedes said, "Give me the right place to stand and I'll move the world." It's the same with research. Once you've asked the right questions, clarity and profits will be close behind.

Much of the effort that large companies put into research is in learning the questions that they can rely upon to be predictive of the actions customers will take. For example, assume that the results of a survey show that 90 percent of customers surveyed said they would buy more if prices were lowered, but 30 percent said they would buy more if customer service were improved. Would you lower prices or improve customer service?

It's hard to know if you also didn't ask customers how much they'd be spending with you. If you learned that the lower-price group would spend an average of $100 more in the next 12 months while the customer-service group would spend $1,000 more in the next 12 months, you'd probably be inclined to put your major effort behind improving customer service.

Asking the right questions is of seminal importance. In conducting thousands of focus groups for many companies, and particularly for direct marketers and catalog companies, I have learned that what people say and how they behave can be quite different. It's not that they lie. It's that they don't know or don't remember why they behaved the way they did and, when asked, give cursory or superficial top-of-mind responses.

Take for example the following questioning of a woman about buying dresses from a catalog:

Moderator: Would you ever spend $500 on a dress from a catalog?

Respondent: No, I wouldn't. I'd first want to see, try it on and look at the quality and the stitching, so I'd probably go to Saks in the neighborhood if I was going to spend that kind of money.

Moderator: Have you ever purchased an expensive dress, say over $500, from a catalog without first seeing it?

Respondent: Well, yes. I bought a Calvin Klein dress.

Moderator: Why would you spend so much for a Calvin Klein dress?

Respondent: Because I've bought enough of the Calvin Klein brand in the past to know the quality of their products. They also fit my figure perfectly. If I'm familiar with the brand and how it fits me, now that I think of it, I guess I'd take a chance ordering expensive dresses from catalogs.

This is a case where the respondent's initial answer shouldn't be characterized as a lie. Rather it's a case of giving a quick response to the wrong question. Had the moderator taken the first response as the answer and not probed further, the catalog company might have been discouraged from upgrading its product line by carrying well-known high-priced brands. The right approach in this case would have been, "Please tell me what dress brands you have purchased from a catalog where you have spent over $500 and tell me why you did so."

Experienced researchers never take consumers' initial responses at face value. *The real truth is usually buried, and it takes skill, thoughtfulness and patience to tease it out.*

And so it goes. The more you learn about your customer motivations, the more insightful and meaningful are the questions that you can ask. Reconciling what consumers think with how they behave is usually the key to asking the right questions.

ATTITUDES VERSUS BEHAVIOR

One of the hardest tasks in research is to understand that consumers don't often give you the whole answer. On one hand, they'll tell you their favorite place to shop for groceries is a certain nearby store, but on the other hand they'll travel miles each week to shop at a different one. Or they may say they love a certain vitamin-rich breakfast cereal but purchase a sugar-coated one three times more frequently.

What consumers think and say must constantly be tempered with how they behave and act. Research is about asking consumers how they feel about companies, products, and services, but it's also about reconciling their attitudes with how they actually behave. Sometimes you'll find that those with the highest opinions of one company behave by purchasing most frequently from a competitor. And, conversely, those with the lowest opinions of another company may give them the lion's share of their business.

Critics of market research have a compelling argument when they say that consumers don't know what they want and, therefore, can't be much help in predicting future trends. The way a lot of research is usually practiced does indeed focus more on what is happening in the present. That doesn't mean, though, that creative research approaches aren't available for better anticipating future trends. As you read Chapter 9 on focus groups, you'll get some ideas for conducting research that is better at predicting trends.

But it isn't always about predicting the future so much as it is about describing the present. Research, indeed, does a good job describing present attitudes and, in doing so, provides a strong road map for planning marketing strategies. For Guerrillas, this can become a major advantage in carving out a more successful and profitable business.

As researchers, we are getting better at knowing when consumer attitudes alone might be incomplete or misleading and when it's prudent to temper attitudes being heard by observing actual behavior. The research steps necessary for reconciling attitudes and behavior aren't that complex, but they do require patience and a substantial financial commitment. But 80 percent to 90 percent of what Guerrillas need to know to improve their business will be provided by sticking to basic research approaches and by uncovering the important attitudes. These are pretty good odds when 50:50 might be the best you could expect otherwise.

DETERMINING THE BEST RESEARCH APPROACH FROM THE OPTIONS AVAILABLE

There are only so many ways to collect research information. There are focus groups or other qualitative approaches; there are phone, mail, internet, shopping-center mall intercept, and panel research methods; and, on rare occasions, personal interviewing in homes or places of business is a method for collecting quantitative survey data.

Choosing which of these approaches, or methodologies, is most desirable is the first hurdle in conducting effective research. Sometimes the best approach is obvious. Other times there are a number of factors that must be considered before settling on the best approach. When deciding on the right methodology, consider the following:

- *Is it easy to determine the right questions to ask?* Often the right line of questioning isn't obvious and it is necessary to conduct some preliminary qualitative research before moving on to the major portion of the research effort.
- *Should the research be projectable, or is getting a feel for issues enough?* Results from focus groups provide a "feel," but they are not projectable and should not be used to represent the opinions shared by everyone. Focus group research will help frame the issues more effectively and can be a very prudent first stop. Once in a great while, the results from focus groups are adequate and further research is unnecessary.
- *How easy or difficult is it getting to customers or prospects whose opinions are important?* For widely used products (e.g., toilet tissue, coffee, soft drinks, checking accounts, automobiles, and computers), it is easy and inexpensive to locate target consumers in order to interview them. For narrowly used products (e.g., men who use hair dye, homeowners who have home movie theaters, diabetics who use insulin), interviewing is more costly because of the difficulty in locating qualified respondents.
- *Once a target respondent is identified, how costly will it be to interview respondents with the right qualifications?* Perhaps older or younger respondents should be interviewed. Maybe it's important to interview only heavy users of a product or only light users. Or perhaps the research should be narrowly focused to users of a particular brand or users who used the product within the past 10 days. These are all factors to be considered in the cost of the study and determining the right approach.
- *How is the information best collected?* Will the questionnaire be long and/or is it necessary to show exhibits or pictures in order to generate meaningful information? Because it's difficult to keep respondents on the phone for more than 20 minutes, conducting the study by mail might be the best approach if you have 40 minutes' worth of questions.
- *Which methodology will produce a valid sample?* It is a constant research challenge to produce a valid sample of target respondents. If the research calls for collecting data from 300 customers, the question becomes how to best locate, gain cooperation and interview a valid random selection of those respondents.
- *Which approach generates a valid sample?* A valid research study must generate a sample of randomly generated target respondents. While it

might be easy and inexpensive to collect 300 interviews using the mail, the question of whether a mail methodology produces a valid sample must be considered.

- *How quickly must the research be completed?* Certain methodologies take much longer to complete (e.g., mail studies). But other methodologies, while faster, might not address all the research objectives. Timing frequently dictates the best approach.
- *What is the research budget?* Certain research methodologies are far more expensive than others. While the most expensive methodology might be the right one, it may be unaffordable and so compromise is necessary. Getting to a budget that is affordable and still provides the necessary information is usually an important issue.

These are some of the issues a researcher must consider when determining the right research approach. While they may seem complex and over-whelming, they often require little more than a working knowledge of research. After completing this book, revisit this section. You should then be able to deal with each and every area with dispatch.

WHICH COMES FIRST?

In a perfect marketing world, a study that provides data for determining *strategic* direction for the company, brand, or product would precede any other kind of research. Remember, without knowing your destination, no road will get you there. At some point, smart marketers will conduct the strategic research necessary to understand how they can compete most effectively.

Often, though, a smaller *tactical* study is the most appropriate initial research effort. Maybe there is a variety of new product ideas or services being considered. Perhaps customer traffic is down or less money is being spent per order. There might be a question regarding the effectiveness of the advertising and what it's communicating. Whatever the situation, tactical research that is limited and narrow in its scope might be the best first step for a small company when beginning to understand the value of research.

What is interesting about tactical research is that results invariably lead to insights that were unanticipated. Focus groups that are intended to shed light on the clarity of advertising might raise issues as to the company's overall marketing approach. For example, a customer in a focus group might say, "The advertising tells me that the products in their stores are the lowest price. That's OK but the reason I really go to them is their great service. I'd even spend a little more with them if they reminded me about their great service."

In this example, if the advertising were intended to communicate a low-price message it would be seen as successful. But now the more strategic issue of stressing customer service rather than price has been raised.

A research consultant might suggest that setting long-term marketing goals should be a first priority and, therefore, strategic research is indicated. Practically, though, a small tactical study that addresses a pressing problem is an equally valid beginning.

What's important to remember is not to jump to conclusions about broad, far-reaching company direction from small studies that are limited in scope.

DETERMINING WHETHER THE PRODUCT MEETS CUSTOMER EXPECTATIONS

A very good research priority is determining the extent to which the products you sell or the services you offer meet customers' needs and expectations. The market is littered with thousands of products that have come and gone. The reason that they fail is often quite simple. Other products come along that deliver better, deliver more, or deliver more cheaply.

Service Merchandise went out of business after discounters like Wal-Mart and Target proved that they could deliver the same products more cheaply and more conveniently. Air Wick lost a huge share of the air-freshener market when Glade introduced more design-friendly dispensers. Sperry-Rand went into free fall while watching mini-computers steal the market from bulky, cumbersome, and costly mainframes.

Conversely, understanding changing times will serve you well. Consumer-goods companies like Gillette and Kellogg's are constantly creating new products that address needs and wants that consumers never thought they had. That is, companies create products in the hope that consumers will find them technologically superior or deliver a benefit that, for whatever reason, will capture consumers' imaginations.

Take TV dinners and the market for convenience foods. We're far beyond the days when consumer needs for a convenient meal were met by popping a TV dinner into the oven. The auto makers are appealing wisely to older customers through the introduction of the retro PT Cruiser and the redesigned Mustang. Look at Apple's iPod, which has taken the playing of music to a whole new level and created a cult-like following in doing so.

Failing to keep up with the needs, wants, wishes, and desires of the marketplace is the best way to lose customers as well as minimize the opportunity to attract new ones. And in failing to create products and services that address consumer needs and wants that don't currently exist or that consumers don't even know they have until presented with the new products, you will also find yourself playing catch-up with a more aggressive competitor. Whatever you might sell, research ensures that you stay current and relevant to the market.

TRACKING CUSTOMER SATISFACTION

Assuming that you have a good fix on where your company is headed and you know that what you sell is relevant, you can turn your attention to how well you are doing the job.

Customer satisfaction for companies selling products through grocery stores is more narrowly focused than customer satisfaction for companies that touch consumers directly. P&G, General Foods, Kraft, Coca-Cola, and Frito-Lay generally judge customer satisfaction by customer acceptance of their products.

Catalog companies and internet marketers, banks, financial institutions, and retailers have sales associates and customer service people who are in constant contact with customers and prospects. They are judged strongly by the levels of customer service they provide, as well as the products they sell.

Tracking the levels of customer satisfaction achieved is particularly important for companies that touch the public directly. Because there is so much competition for catalog, internet, and retail shoppers' money, losing business because of sloppy, underperforming, or inadequate customer service is unforgivable. It is important to remember that, in general, it costs seven times as much to attract a new customer as it does to keep a current customer.

Spending money to ensure that you keep those customers you already have should be your top research priority. A reliable customer satisfaction study needn't be expensive and will serve as the cornerstone for growing your business.

IS YOUR MESSAGE BEING HEARD?

There was a company called Micro-Switch. They sold large, expensive switching equipment to telephone companies. Their customers were highly skilled, highly technical purchasing agents. Every year, Micro-Switch spent about $2,500,000 advertising in technical journals. Year after year, their advertising message stressed their wide product line. One year, they raised the issue of whether anyone read their ads or even knew about the many products they sold.

Several market research studies determined that most purchasing agents couldn't recall seeing their advertising. Those who did said they knew that Micro-Switch had a wide product line, but they didn't know much else about the company. They were unaware of how the company serviced the products it sold or the technical expertise its salespeople brought to customers planning to purchase switching equipment. Further, they said it was important that these areas were addressed before they'd ever call the company in for consultation.

This is a case of a company spending millions from their advertising budget on messages that not only weren't being heard but failed to communicate in a relevant way. The cost of the research was $30,000.

I'm continually amazed that companies will routinely spend hundreds of thousands or millions of dollars on advertising and not spend a small fraction of that to determine whether what they are saying is being heard or whether it communicates an important message.

In considering your research priorities, consider what you spend on advertising, direct mail, sales promotion, public relations, telemarketing, or other special events and ask yourself whether the money is being well spent. If you don't know the answer, research can help.

GENERATING MORE BUSINESS FROM CURRENT CUSTOMERS

Again, when setting research priorities, it's wise to first allocate funds to study current customers. Assuming, then, that you are doing a good job with your customers, your next opportunity for growth is to sell more to those customers.

The relationship current customers have with a company makes them more predisposed to listen when the company has something to say. It's far easier to encourage current customers to purchase additional products in the product line, purchase the same products more often, try new products, or take greater advantage of services you offer than it is to find totally new customers.

How you generate more business from current customers is, of course, dependent on what you sell. But assuming that you have the potential to sell them more, determining which customer groups have the greatest potential for additional sales efforts becomes important.

If you have a catalog or internet business, a current customer might be one who has purchased from you in the past 30, 60, or 90 days or even beyond. If you are selling automobiles, home décor, or other less frequently purchased products, you might be inclined to define a current customer as having purchased in the past year or two years.

There is no pat definition or time period for defining a current customer. It must be done using common sense and an analysis of your current customer database – presuming, of course, that there is a customer database you can access that captures such information. However you define current customers, you must realistically determine the period of time after which it is safe to assume that there is potential for selling to the customer again.

Take a company such as Cabela's, which has a fishing, hunting, and outdoor-products catalog. Cabela's might define a current customer as having made at least one purchase from its catalog or website within the past 30 days. Research and live testing might also prove that it receives the best return on its marketing expenditures if it appeals more strongly to past-30-day buyers. The company might also know that appealing to the past-60- or past-90-day buyers produces profitable returns, although less so. And appealing to buyers beyond 90 days is unprofitable.

Therefore, Cabela's could define past-30-day buyers as current best customers, 31- to 90-day buyers as current good customers, and buyers beyond 90 days as inactive customers. In setting market research priorities, Cabela's might determine that understanding what it has to do to sell more to its best and good customers would likely generate the most immediate return.

For inactive customers, it would be important for Cabela's to understand attitudes toward the company and issues that must be addressed so that the relationship can be reinvigorated. And for prospects, or those who have never purchased at all, understanding the hurdles to an initial purchase might dictate that Cabela's take yet a totally different approach.

Each time you identify a customer or prospect target, you allow for the likelihood that attitudes and perceptions will differ from one target to the next and that the marketing actions indicated for one target will be different from those indicated for another. And remember, it can be a waste of money to study a variety of targets at one time when you are unable to take different actions for the different targets.

TAKING CUSTOMERS AWAY FROM THE COMPETITION

In determining your list of research priorities, studying what it takes to attract customers from competitors should come when you have shored up your relationship with current customers. That isn't to suggest that attracting competitors' customers is unimportant. Rather, there is no point in spending advertising or promotion budgets or sales-force efforts to lure your competitors' customers only to quickly lose them. Once you have done your homework and determined that your products or services address the needs of your current customers, you can begin to think about research to attract new customers.

In seeking to attract your competitors' customers, the same kinds of research studies that you'd use when studying your own customers apply. Here, though, your target respondents will include your competitors' customers and so will provide intelligence regarding your competitors' strengths and weaknesses. Such research will become a road map to the kinds of strategies that would be effective for determining which competitors are the most vulnerable and the messages that would be most compelling in convincing a competitor's customers to switch to you.

INCREASING THE SIZE OF THE MARKET

In the scheme of things, attracting new users to your market is the hardest task. The hurdles necessary to convince prospects that buying what you sell is in their interest are often substantial. For example, consumers who haven't purchased packaged low-calorie foods or have failed to buy exercise equipment for use in their home may be a much tougher sell for those products than consumers who have purchased those products in the past.

It is also important to realize that, when you seek to grow the market, you are doing so not only for yourself but for your competitors. It is doubly tough to attract new users to the marketplace while at the same time convincing them that they should purchase your products instead of those of your competitors.

Take Apple and the iPod. Apple has been phenomenally successful in creating the market for digital music. While Apple will undoubtedly pay attention to protecting its position, it won't be a walk in the park. The same is true for any marketer who seeks to create a new or bigger market.

5

How much does research cost?

Budgeting for research is not a precise science. There are a number of guide-lines practiced by large companies that could be considered in setting your research budget. They include:

1. *Allocating a percentage for research out of the overall marketing budget.* If a company spends $50 million on marketing programs, anywhere from 0.5 percent ($250,000) to 5 percent ($2,500,000) might be allocated to research. In the case of companies such as Kraft or General Foods, where there are many different brands, the research is generally allotted per brand using the above percentage ranges.
2. *Allocating a percentage of the advertising budget.* Sometimes the advertising budget alone is used in allocating research funds. If a company spends $25 million on advertising, the same percentages as above are used to allocate research dollars.
3. *Allocating a percentage of sales.* Some companies, particularly industrial or manufacturing companies that don't have substantial marketing or advertising budgets, often allocate research as a percentage of sales. Anywhere from 0.5 percent to 1 percent is typical.
4. *Assessing needs.* A popular method to determine research allocation is to list the projects that should be undertaken in the coming year and assign dollar figures to each project. An initial list is usually reviewed by those who will use the research results. This could be any number of people in the company, or perhaps the company's vendors might lend their expertise. From this collaborative review, projects are added that are believed necessary or eliminated where felt unnecessary.

5. *Ad hoc.* In large companies, the bane of a researcher's existence is the need to convince the holder of the budget to allocate funds ad hoc each and every time a research issue surfaces. In such instances, there may be a research budget that is allocated, but the researcher is constantly forced to justify the use of the funds. This isn't necessarily bad, as it forces the researcher to consider whether the research is really needed and whether the cost will produce actionable results. The problem with ad hoc research is that it doesn't provide a strong strategic-thinking focus regarding the forward-thinking issues that need to be addressed to grow the company or brand. When conducting ad hoc research, issues tend to be tactical in nature and responsive to immediate problems and, therefore, low-impact decision making.

6. *Some combination of the above.* Often, a firm research budget is agreed upon that will accommodate a number of strategic and tactical studies for the coming year. Additionally, there is an ad hoc "slush fund" that is available when unexpected issues arise throughout the year and research is indicated.

7. *No research budget at all.* This is akin to ad hoc budgeting, with many companies not allocating a research budget at all. In such cases, the budget might be in the hands of the president, director of marketing, or brand, product or advertising management. Research is then undertaken only when management feels the need is particularly strong.

Whichever budgeting process is used, it is important that a degree of flexibility should exist. No one can predict with complete certainty whether every research project that might be planned in a November budgeting process will be necessary the following June.

Likewise, many priority issues surface throughout the year that cannot be anticipated and become a priority. What is ultimately important in research budgeting is that a commitment be made to improve decision making by spending research dollars. It is then incumbent upon the company to decide which budgeting process is the best to follow to that end.

DETERMINING A MEANINGFUL RESEARCH BUDGET

For small companies and entrepreneurs, research is one of the last things they think they can afford. Mostly, research is viewed as a highly discretionary expense, one that is difficult to justify because research costs aren't easily attributable to immediate paybacks.

The owner of a small manufacturing company once said to me, "If I spend $50,000 on research, will I get $100,000 back?" I responded, "If you don't spend the money on research, how will you know that you won't ultimately waste $500,000 advertising your product using the wrong message?"

Another said, "I could hire two salespeople for the cost of your research. If I do that, I know how much in sales and profit I can expect." My response was "Maybe you should hire one salesperson and spend money you would have paid the second to learn about your customers and why they aren't buying more from you. In this way you can help the salespeople you now have be more effective. It just might be that, if your salespeople were better informed, their selling efforts would increase dramatically."

Trusting the process is always in question the first time money is spent on research. The vague hope always exists that the results will lead to smarter decisions, which will increase sales and profits that would not have happened otherwise. This makes it all the more critical that great care be taken in planning the research and anticipating the kind of actions that will be taken when the research is completed.

It is also important to realize that research might suggest action should not be taken. When considering a new venture or change of course, there are always costs associated with the risk. Often, research will indicate that an idea is not worth pursuing or that the money necessary to do the job effectively might be beyond company means. In such cases, the payback from the research is the prevention of costly mistakes.

In essence, then, a meaningful research budget is whatever it takes to get the job done – to get the information needed for making wiser decisions. Sometimes it can be as little as several thousand dollars. Rarely will an initial research plunge be more than $25,000. And, realistically, a meaningful year-long program is likely to approach six figures.

Another important budgeting factor is whether you conduct the research yourself, thus saving the costs associated with using research suppliers or consultants. This is a decision that should be made only after completing this book.

COMING TO GRIPS WITH A BUDGET

There are three scenarios that are usually in play when determining research budgets. They are:

1. "First project look-see" budget;
2. "It feels about right" budget;
3. "Let's do it right" budget.

The "first project look-see"

This approach is applicable for companies that have never spent money on research. They might determine that a problem persists after attempting to solve it in any number of ways. Or an issue might cry for fresh thinking and a different perspective, and research is looked to for solutions.

"Let's toss some money at it and maybe we'll learn something" is the scenario that is part and parcel of the first project look-see. The fact is that first-time research users often come to the research on a wing and a prayer. That is not to say that this is bad. Getting to any point where research is given an opportunity is a big step forward.

Focus groups are clearly the most popular research approach for first-time users. Frequently they feel that getting new customers is their biggest problem and the one that they want to research. And, undoubtedly, there will be some surprise when they learn what a simple focus group study can cost.

But, whatever barriers must be overcome, first-time users tend not to look beyond the results of the first project. Although they feel it necessary to take an unbiased look at a particularly nagging problem, they tend to have their fingers crossed that their money will be well spent.

If you are a first project look-see company, you should plan on spending a minimum of $20,000 with an outside research company on that first project. Otherwise, save your money. But, if you think you can do the same project without outside help, cut that figure in half.

"It feels about right"

Perhaps you are trying to set a 12-month research budget. You can look at company sales and take an industry percentage (anywhere from 0.5 percent to 2 percent of sales) to determine a research budget. You can allocate a percentage of your marketing or advertising budget. Or you can do almost any other kind of number crunching to come up with a figure.

But new research users trying to set a research budget tend to do so on a "feels right" basis.

Most likely there will have been some success with a first project look-see, and research is now being viewed as a potentially valuable ongoing tool. The company will regard research more as a series of projects than as an occasional here-and-there project – as a tool to bring a more disciplined approach into decision making.

Committing to any kind of yearly research budget is a big step. And arriving at a specific figure will probably require a series of compromises.

Since the money must come from somewhere, it becomes a give-and-take process. Perhaps less is budgeted for salary increases, new equipment or R&D. Maybe it is determined that the money should come straight from the bottom line.

In deciding how to budget, listen to Gerry Linda's thought:

> One of the best reasons to conduct market research is that it is a form of low-cost business insurance. You can insure your company against making a big mistake – even an enterprise threatening mistake – by the judicious research study. You may cancel a bad idea or forget about a new product you're hot on. Remember that nine out of 10 new products fail and you are not likely to beat the odds if you don't do some research.

Whatever rationale is ultimately followed, a yearly research budget of $100,000 is realistic and should generate three to five meaningful studies. If you think you can conduct those studies without outside help, cut that figure by 40 to 50 percent.

"Let's do it right"

Setting a research budget on the basis of company goals is usually the best way to go. If you choose this route, use a professional researcher in the budgeting process. Explore what you are trying to accomplish in the next 12 months and focus on the areas where research can help you achieve your goals. Consider both strategic and tactical issues. Make a wish list of projects that you'd like to do.

By retaining a research professional in this process, you'll probably be happy to discover that one large strategic research study will support a wide range of research goals and be less costly than a series of smaller ones. You also might find it to be more economical to wait to conduct tactical studies until you have the materials available to combine several into one.

And, again, as with any budgeting process, you'll no doubt have to make compromises. But if you choose the "do it right" approach, you'll have come to the realization that research is essential to the way you conduct your business. And, as a result, you will find that the money you budgeted for research, whatever the amount, can be spent better than you imagined.

Of course, it depends on the size of your company and your resources, but doing research the right way is likely to produce a research budget reaching beyond six figures.

WHAT BUSINESS ARE YOU IN?

Your research budget can be determined by the scope and size of your business.

Manufacturing companies have a more limited customer and prospect base to study than do consumer package-goods companies. Small local or regional companies have a far more limited geographic customer base to consider than do national companies.

And, irrespective of your business, there is a price tag associated with each potential target that you might research. Here are some likely targets that any business could study:

1. Studying current customers could necessitate including targets such as those who:
   - are your best or most profitable customers compared to those who are your worst or most unprofitable;
   - may have purchased once in the recent past but not a second time;
   - were heavy purchasers in the recent past but stopped buying;
   - currently purchase from you but also purchase a substantial amount from your competitors;
   - first came to your company as a result of various sales efforts (e.g., salesperson solicitation, direct mail/internet solicitation, telemarketing solicitation, referral, etc.).
2. Studying your competitors' customers would include targets that might:
   - have purchased from you a year ago or more but are no longer active customers;
   - be highly satisfied or dissatisfied with your competitors;
   - have purchased from more than one of your competitors, but have not considered purchasing from you.
3. Studying non-buyers in your product category could include those who:
   - have purchased in your product category but have done so long ago;
   - have never purchased in your product category but whom you determine to have a higher probability of buying as against those who have a lower probability of ever buying.

While the scope and size of your business will determine how much you can afford to invest, the business that you are in should have little influence in determining where you place your research priorities. What you will find is that from year to year, as your learning increases, you'll dig deeper. Research targets that today don't seem to offer much payback become the ones that tomorrow will offer the best potential for growth.

6

Using research professionals

Should Guerrillas try this at home? Maybe! What I do know is that a good research professional is worth his or her weight in gold. But if you have the time and interest to learn what it takes to do effective research, there is no reason you can't execute the studies yourself at a fraction of the cost it would take to use a professional. *At the least, you can determine those areas in which you don't feel qualified and when employing a research consultant on a limited basis would be prudent.*

Assuming that you would hire a professional for at least some of your research, the remainder of this chapter will help you locate the best person or company. If you are intent on conducting your research yourself, this chapter will not be of much help to you in achieving that goal.

HOW TO JUDGE CREDENTIALS

The American Marketing Association (www.marketingpower.com) is the primary association for professional marketing researchers. The AMA lists more than 38,000 member companies and more than 750,000 individual members. There are over 1,100 market research suppliers listed as members. In looking at the Chicago business-to-business *Yellow Pages*, there are more than 225 listings under the heading "Market Research and Analysis." If you really want to investigate the options beyond this, go to Google, type in "market research companies", and start scanning the millions of listings.

In Western Europe, Asia, and Latin America, there are also many professional research organizations. In Europe, for example, you can access www.esomar.org, www.aemri.org, or www.efamro.org and find thousands of professional marketing research companies and field services. If you want to conduct research in Asia, Latin America, or Eastern Europe, simply go on Google and type in "marketing research organizations" preceded by your country of interest (e.g., "Asia marketing research organizations") and you'll find all the resources you need.

There is no shortage of market research suppliers or individual research consultants available to assist you in your research effort. The trick comes in finding sources that are best for you. To find them and pay them the least amount of money to help you, follow these guidelines:

1. *Find a smaller research supplier.* Even a one-person research supplier or consultant would be good. Individuals who work out of their homes have little overhead to consider when pricing their services. It should be no surprise that the bigger the research company, the more overhead will go into the pricing of its projects.

2. *Check credentials.* Obviously, looking at a research supplier's website or reading its literature will tell you what services it offers. But it won't tell you much about whether the company is right for you. It's not as much about the supplier you hire as it is about the person working on your studies. If the supplier looks like it's for you, phone up, explain your situation and ask to speak to the person who would work on your business.

3. *Meet the supplier personally.* If a telephone conversation gives you a good feeling about the researcher, request a personal meeting. But, prior to that meeting, ask for a résumé or biography of the person(s) you'd be working with as well as a client list with the names and phone numbers of references you can contact. You want to ensure that:

   – The person you'd work with has at least 10 years of experience. While somewhat less might be OK, make sure that you are dealing with someone who has been around long enough to have seen a wide variety of problems. It is reasonable to expect a researcher at a large supplier to be involved in at least 50 projects per year. Having 10 years of experience will likely have exposed a person to whatever issues you might be facing. If you are considering a one-person shop, you definitely want a 10-plus-year veteran of the research business.

   – The person has some experience in your line of business. If you are a retail business, you probably don't want someone whose career has focused on conducting research for food or beverage companies. If you are selling technology-related products, you would be prudent to find someone who has a technical education and/or research experience with technology companies. Personally, I believe it is beneficial to find a researcher who has worked for one of your competitors. Whether consciously or not, the researcher will use that wealth of experience to make your project better.

- You hire someone with user-side experience. If you are considering a one-person supplier or consultant, make sure he or she has previous experience in the research department of a large company or advertising agency research department. Both backgrounds will provide in-depth knowledge in translating your marketing problems to marketing research objectives and ultimately to effective market research methodologies. Hiring a researcher who has had only supplier-side experience should be done cautiously. Many have a limited perspective in translating marketing objectives to market research objectives. So make sure that the supplier you hire has served clients in both consulting and project execution capacities.

- The person should have worked for more than one company. If you find someone who knows only the Kraft, General Foods, P&G, or Microsoft way of doing research, you are likely to get very-big-company research solutions to your problem. Further, if a researcher has worked only in very large companies, his or her perspective might be limited. Large-company researchers are certainly smart people, but someone from Kraft or P&G will likely approach your project with a big budget in mind. The perfect combination would be a person who has worked in research for small, medium- and large-sized companies.

- The person is an all-around researcher. Some researchers know only how to conduct focus groups and couldn't write a survey questionnaire to save their lives. Others have experience only in certain kinds of research (e.g., product testing, advertising testing, segmentation research), giving them a limited perspective.

Mostly importantly, you don't want an individual who is likely to fit only the methodologies he or she knows into your problem.

Hiring a professor

If you can find a teacher or professor of marketing research at a nearby college or university, you might have stumbled on to something. I am not talking here about a professor of marketing, but about a professor of marketing research.

It usually takes some practical experience to be a good teacher of research. Those who gravitate to teaching often have rich and varied backgrounds that include a great deal of practical experience. And professors generally charge less for their time than research professionals. Just make sure you follow the guidelines above when you consider hiring a professor as your research supplier. The last thing you want is an egghead who will wow you with academic jargon and recommend impractical textbook approaches.

ARE RESEARCH SUPPLIERS OR CONSULTANTS REALLY ALL THAT NECESSARY?

You can become a reasonably good researcher if you have the time and interest, just as you can become a pretty good copywriter, producer of TV commercials, photographer of models for ads, or accountant for your company taxes. The trick is not to move too fast or waste money by getting in over your head.

Over a reasonable period of time, you can learn to conduct an effective focus group, write an insightful questionnaire, deal with field services that collect data, engage firms to tabulate your data, and become good at interpreting results. But you'll probably waste a lot of time and money if you try it all at once.

If you have found someone you trust and think that person can help you, learn how to get his or her services at the most affordable price.

UNDERSTANDING SUPPLIER PRICING

When "buying" research, it is important to know something about the process. In general, there are two types of research companies. There are *full-service research suppliers* that primarily provide problem definition, research objective definition, project execution and control and analytical services. And there are *field-service suppliers* whose primary function is to provide data-collection services to full-service suppliers. In this instance, full-service suppliers provide project specifications to the field-service suppliers. This includes the type of study being conducted, the anticipated length of the questionnaire to be completed, the profile and number of respondents to be interviewed, and the manner in which data are to be collected.

Field-service suppliers, in turn, price their work to the full-service suppliers. The full-service suppliers make a large percentage of their profits by marking up field-service costs. If you become the direct client of the field-service supplier, you will save this markup. You should also know that field-service suppliers realize that they are often facing a competitor's bid. Therefore, most will negotiate price – at least somewhat.

There are a number of research suppliers that are full-service and have their own data-collection field-service arm. These tend to be very large companies, eg The Gallup Organization, J.D. Powers and Associates, and The Roper Company. These are highly reputable research organizations that tend to service Fortune 1000 companies. They have far higher overhead costs, which must be passed on in the pricing of their projects. For smaller companies and entrepreneurs, using these companies is often unaffordable and unnecessary.

COSTING A PROJECT

When full-service research suppliers price their projects, 50 percent or more of the cost of the project usually goes to the consultant's field-service suppliers, not to the consultant's bank account. In the case of focus groups or other qualitative research projects the consultant will incur out-of-pocket costs to field services for:

- renting a facility where the focus groups will be conducted;
- recruiting costs for the field service to screen the right respondents and make sure that they show up at the right time;
- monetary incentives to respondents for participating;
- miscellaneous costs such as respondent and client food, videotaping, or other material costs necessary to complete the project.

In the case of a survey, the consultant will pay field services for:

- the professional interviewers they provide for screening likely respondents and administering the questionnaire to the desired number of respondents;
- line charges associated with phone studies, mall charges associated with collecting data in a shopping center, mail charges associated with conducting a study by mail, or internet costs associated with programming an online questionnaire and setting up the website;
- monetary incentives that might be required to ensure respondent cooperation in the research;

- charges for having the questionnaires tabulated;
- charges for statistical procedures that might be necessary when analyzing the data.

If you choose to work directly with field services, you should be ready to tell them exactly what you want them to do. Rarely, if ever, would you use a field service for professional advice on how to conduct or analyze a study. Field-service personnel don't generally have experience in designing or analyzing research data. They are, first and foremost, suppliers of respondents and are best used when told exactly what should be accomplished.

If you wanted to become a full-service researcher supplier, you would find it very easy to do because all you would have to do is put out a sign that says, "I'm a research supplier," and find a client who believes you. To price a study, then, all you need do is determine what you want your field services to do and how much you have to pay them to provide you with the number of interviews you need for your research. With that information in hand, plus a few other smaller out-of-pocket costs, you would simply decide how much more you want to charge your client for the project.

DO ALL RESEARCH SUPPLIERS PRICE THEIR PROJECTS THE SAME WAY?

No. And to get the most for your research expenditure, it is necessary to understand supplier pricing. Only by knowing the elements that go into a study can you determine if you are getting good value or being ripped off. Essentially, market research can be purchased from a supplier in two ways.

First, it can be purchased as a *fixed-cost project*. Fixed-cost projects are all-inclusive. That is, the supplier will quote you one cost, which will include fees for helping you define your research objectives, developing a questionnaire for a survey or discussion guide for conducting focus groups, collecting data, analyzing results, and making recommendations.

A fixed-cost quote will also include the supplier's out-of-pocket costs to their field services. These include costs for field services that conduct the actual interviewing for your project, for the tabulation company that will array the data so that they can be analyzed, for a statistician if special statistical procedures are necessary, and for any other costs associated with completing the project (e.g., copy and printing services, preparing necessary exhibits, etc.).

Fixed-price costing is the most popular approach for full-service research suppliers. Because it is virtually impossible for a research buyer to know how much markup and profit are in a fixed-price bid, the only way to know if you are paying more than you should is to get competitive bids. If you get a lower bid from a second company, you might be satisfied that you have been given a good price. In reality, though, all it means is that the second company is more competitive on its pricing. It doesn't necessarily mean that you are getting the best possible price, as a third supplier could be even less expensive.

Second, market research can be purchased at an *hourly rate plus out-of-pocket expense costs*. Here, the supplier will give you hourly rates for the various services. Some suppliers charge the same hourly rate no matter what the task. Others will charge one rate for their time involved in problem definition and research objective setting, another rate for questionnaire development, another for quality control, and yet another for analyzing the data and developing recommendations. They will then provide you with an estimate of the hours and costs necessary for their services plus the out-of-pocket costs that they would pay their field services and other suppliers.

Given this approach to costing, you know exactly what you are paying in out-of-pocket costs and professional services. This makes it much easier to judge whether one company charges more for its services than another. And while some suppliers are certainly worth more than others, you'll at least have a level playing field when making a decision.

As I said, the vast majority of research suppliers would prefer to work on a fixed-cost basis. Usually, fixed-cost pricing will produce greater revenue than hourly pricing. In fact, some research suppliers refuse to quote hourly rates for their services because it exposes their markup structure. If you run into a company like this, I would suggest that you stay away from them altogether.

HOW MUCH WILL A MODERATOR MAKE ON A FOCUS GROUP PROJECT?

Let's start with fixed-cost pricing and look at a focus group project.

A typical focus group consists of four two-hour focus group sessions. The average out-of-pocket costs a supplier will pay a field service if they are conducting a "run of the mill" focus group study will be roughly as shown in Table 6.1.

The average cost a focus group moderator will charge is $2,500 per group, which includes all project planning, moderation, report preparation and recommendations. That comes to $10,000 for a four-group study. The fee quoted to the client, without travel, would be:

Moderator fee	$10,000
Total out-of-pocket costs	$9,100
Total fixed-price quote	**$19,100**

This $19,100 cost is subject to a number of upward or downward swings. Some moderators charge far more than $2,500 per group. Many have a going fee that can be upward of $4,000, particularly moderators from a large city such as New York, Chicago or Los Angeles. Of course, some will charge less than $2,500 depending on their workload, their relationship with the client, their likelihood of leveraging the study into additional studies, or their level of experience. Further, moderators may be inclined to take a markup, in the 20 percent range, on the fees charged by their field services. This would add another $1,800 or so to the above project cost.

Moderators will also make additional money on the respondent incentives they've budgeted. In the previous example, $3,000 was budgeted for incentives for 40 respondents. Rarely will the moderator have to pay out the whole $3,000 as it is unlikely that all 40 respondents will show up. If only eight show for each group, it means that only $2,400 in incentives will be paid out. Be aware, though, that it is the rare moderator who will rebate that $600 savings to the client.

Also, field-service costs can vary considerably, given the type of respondent to be interviewed. Professional focus groups, such as those conducted with company officers, purchasing agents, medical doctors, lawyers, stockbrokers, etc., are far more costly to recruit and the incentive that these respondents receive is far higher than that for a "normal" respondent. Other hard-to-locate groups, such as buyers of particular brands, users of products that are rarely purchased, or extremely high-income consumers, are also more costly.

Table 6.1 Example of out-of-pocket focus group costs

	Costs	$
1.	Focus group room rental – 4 groups @ $450/group	1,800
2.	Recruiting respondents – 10 recruits/group at $100 per recruit for a total of 40 recruits	4,000
3.	Respondent incentives – 40 respondents @ $75/respondent	3,000
4.	Food and refreshments	300
	Total out-of-pocket costs	**9,100**

SAVING MONEY ON FOCUS GROUP STUDIES

If asked, many moderators will work on an hourly basis and are more than happy to have you pay their field services directly or show you the written cost estimates they receive from the field services. In order to save money on your focus group projects here are a number of suggestions:

1. *Get competitive costs.* Find at least two acceptable moderators and ask for fixed-price competitive quotes.
2. *Ask a third moderator what would be charged by working on an hourly basis.* Have the moderator give you the actual written estimate from at least two focus group field services. Compare the fixed and hourly bids and be prepared for a pleasant surprise.
3. *Have both the fixed-cost and hourly moderators quote costs for both a full report and a brief summary.* You can usually get 90 percent of what you need from a summary report, particularly if you view the focus groups yourself and take good notes. If the purpose of your focus group project is to help you write a more effective questionnaire for a follow-up survey, a full report should not be necessary. The moderator should lower fees by about $500 per group if he or she doesn't have to write a report.
4. *Ask the moderator to give you tiered pricing.* Most moderators would be inclined to charge less per group after the first two groups. Particularly in larger focus group studies where six or eight groups are necessary, there could be a substantial saving on the moderator's fee with tiered pricing.
5. *By all means, ask the moderator to rebate the budgeted but unused respondent incentives.*
6. *Determine whether you can conduct your focus groups in smaller, less expensive markets.* In the United States, try to stay out of the very large markets such as New York City, Chicago, Boston, Los Angeles, or San Francisco, where field-service costs tend to be 10 percent to 20 percent higher. Even large markets, such as Atlanta, Milwaukee, Tampa, Nashville, San Antonio, and Sacramento, are often more cost-effective than the major markets cited above. And smaller markets, such as Des Moines, Knoxville, Jacksonville, or Fort Wayne, are even better yet. The same holds true for almost any country around the world. Conducting focus groups in London or Paris, for example, would likely be more expensive than finding a focus group facility in Bath or Lyon. The point is that, the larger the market, the more expensive it will be to conduct focus groups. Therefore, you will save money by avoiding large metropolitan areas if smaller areas are adequate for your objectives.

7. *Determine whether videotaping is necessary.* Many moderators will suggest videotaping focus groups. You should first determine if videotapes would be valuable for you. Sometimes showing the video to people not attending the groups or to give emphasis in a sales or planning meeting is a good idea, and the extra expense is then warranted. In 75 percent of the studies, audiotapes are all that are necessary to analyze results and to ensure a record of groups – and those are provided free of charge by all focus group facilities. You should know that many facilities will charge $50 to $100 to videotape each group, but some will do so free of charge. If you want to videotape, ask the moderator to book your groups only at focus group facilities that give you free videotaping.
8. *Watch your food and refreshment costs.* It always amazes me when I'm charged $50 by a focus group facility for a $15 pizza that my clients will eat while watching the group. Many facilities will take ridiculous markups on the food they provide you or your respondents. Others are happy to bill only the costs that they incur. Be clear on what you are paying for food and refreshments.

HOW MUCH WILL A SUPPLIER MAKE ON A TELEPHONE SURVEY?

The fixed-cost quote that you will receive from a supplier conducting a telephone survey is calculated much like a focus group project. To reiterate, it will consist of three elements:

1. how much the full-service supplier will pay in out-of-pocket costs to the field service and other suppliers;
2. how much you are charged for the supplier's labor and the labor of others in the company who will work on your project;
3. how high the markup will be on 1 and 2.

Here is an example. Assume you had a telephone survey that you wanted to complete with 300 respondents who had eaten at a fast-food restaurant in the past week. Table 6.2 gives an example that is typical of how a full-service research supplier will arrive at your cost quote.

There are a number of major factors that go into this quote that affect the final cost. They are:

1. *How well the supplier has negotiated the out-of-pocket cost with the telephone interviewing services.* The $35 cost per completed interview could be

Table 6.2 Example of survey pricing

Cost component	Cost $
a. *Out-of-pocket cost:*	
Telephone interviewing field service (300 20-minute interviews @ $35 per completed interview)	10,500
Purchase of random sample of phone numbers	900
Tabulation of data	1,000
Statistical analysis (3 regression analyses)	900
Courier delivery	100
Printing report	75
Internal cost allocation for phone, fax, etc.	50
Supplies/other miscellaneous costs	50
Total out-of-pocket cost	**13,575**
b. *Internal labor:*	
Project planning (10 hours @ $150/hour)	1,500
Questionnaire development (10 hours @ $200/hour)	2,000
Field service project management (5 hours at $100/hour)	500
Report and recommendations (25 hours at $250 per hour)	6,250
Total internal labor	**10,250**
Total out-of-pocket plus labor cost (a + b)	**23,825**
Project markup (at 50%)	11,912
Total	**35,737**
Cost quoted to client	**35,700**
Cost per interview ($35,700 divided by 300 interviews)	119

high or low. Obviously, this one cost is a major component of your final price, and there is always the question of whether the consultant has negotiated a strongly competitive price with a quality telephone interviewing service.

2. *The estimate of labor hours and the hourly rates for each function.* Research suppliers don't know with absolute certainty if they will spend more hours on a project than estimated. In a fixed-cost quote, they can be killed by a project that becomes a problem and necessitates additional time that can't be charged to you. This is time that could be spent on other projects for other clients. Because of this, research suppliers tend to overestimate the actual hours needed to complete a project. If they are more efficient than they planned, they will enjoy an unusually high profit on the study.

3. *How their staff is priced.* Hourly staff rates for the tasks necessary to complete a project can vary wildly from supplier to supplier. Some suppliers will have junior staff members work on your project and charge you lower rates. Others will assign senior staff to the project and charge you accordingly. Then, too, some may charge senior staff rates but assign junior people to your project.

4. *The markup.* Larger full-service research companies have greater overhead and must mark up their projects more than smaller companies. The labor rates for larger companies also tend to be higher. While a 50 percent markup is typical for both large and small suppliers, some will mark up 60 percent, while others may mark up only 40 percent or 30 percent. When business is slow, markups tend to go down since suppliers are forced to get projects in the door to cover their fixed overhead and salaries. When business is strong, markups may increase, as the loss of some projects might be a worthwhile risk. Increasing the markup to unsuspecting clients in particularly busy times will certainly result in extraordinary profits.

SAVING MONEY ON YOUR SURVEY

While all this might be interesting, you might be wondering what it means for you. It is very difficult to purchase quality research less expensively if you don't have this background. When you know what you're dealing with, there is no question that you can get a better deal. Follow one or more of the approaches described below the next time you get a cost quote for a survey:

1. *Always get two or three fixed-cost estimates from full-service suppliers that you have screened and feel comfortable using.* The trick is to make sure that all the suppliers are giving you costs for exactly the same project specifications. Although suppliers hate this, it may necessitate taking the specifications of the project you work out with one supplier and giving those exact specifications to other suppliers. If you do this, tell the second supplier that you worked out the methodology with one of their competitors but that you want them to provide competitive costs nevertheless. They will understand and appreciate your honesty. They might even tend to lower their markup because they know they are in a competitive situation. Also tell them that, if they don't agree with the methodology you give them, they should feel free to suggest alternative approaches.

2. *Ask yet another supplier to quote the project but to separate the out-of-pocket costs from the labor costs.* You might find that getting project quotes in this manner will come close to the fixed-price quotes that you received. This is because the supplier simply adds the normal markup into the two costs. But when costing this way, many suppliers tend to charge less for their labor or take less of a markup on their out-of-pocket costs.

3. *Offer to pay 75 percent of the cost of the project up front, and ask for a discount.* Research suppliers, especially the smaller ones, tend to have cash flow issues. When you approve your project, it is normal for the research supplier to invoice you for 50 percent of the contracted cost with 30 days to pay. The remaining 50 percent is billed when you receive the final report and are satisfied. Until your money is received, it might be necessary for your supplier to front a significant portion of your project's expenses. Also, research suppliers may worry about a client's payment history or even their ability to pay. You might consider telling the supplier that you will write a check the day the invoice is received in return for a discount on a project. By showing concern and good faith in this area, you're likely to find research suppliers (particularly the smaller ones) willing to cut you a better deal.

4. *Find a one-person research supplier you trust.* Assuming that the person is not swamped with projects, there is no question that costs will be lower than any you receive from a larger research supplier.

5. *Defer the project.* If you feel that the costs you receive are beyond your budget but you can afford to wait for the research results, ask the supplier if the research might be conducted less expensively when the supplier has more time – say in a month or two.

6. *Consider more than one project.* Think seriously about conducting more than one research study, whether at the same time or with the second several months later. If your supplier is aware that the first project will lead to a second, and you are ready to commit to more than one project, you are likely to get lower costs on both. This is particularly true if you commit to a significant "research budget" for the next 12 months. Like other suppliers and consultants, research suppliers are more interested in long-term relationships than in the money that they make from your one project. Most are willing to take a lower markup when costing several projects than when they are costing only one.

7. *Refer the supplier to another client.* Give the supplier a lead that turns into another client and watch what happens with your final invoice.

8. *Get the 10 percent back.* Research suppliers usually quote their studies plus or minus 10 percent, for example $19,100 +/–10 percent or $35,700 +/–10 percent. Ethical research suppliers would never take the 10 percent contingency without informing you when they run into

unusually high expenses. If during the course of your project unantici-pated costs arise, the research supplier should inform you of the problem. You can then decide if you want to make additional expendi-tures or compromise elsewhere. But it is highly unusual for a supplier to give you back the minus part of the contingency if he or she does better on your project than was estimated. At the end of your project, especially if you are happy and plan to use the supplier again, state that, and ask the supplier's opinion as to how the project turned out. Mention the 10 percent contingency and inquire about the possibility of lowering the final invoice by some percentage.

9. *Offer to pay the research supplier's out-of-pocket expenses directly.* Any financial burden that you will assume might be cause for the research supplier to lower the fees.

ARE RESEARCH SUPPLIERS WORTH WHAT THEY CHARGE?

Unequivocally yes. Unequivocally no.

The larger the research supplier that you use – usually a supplier with more than five people – the more likely you will be to get a junior person working on your business. That means that the person who sold you the project and in whom you have placed all your trust may not be paying as much attention to how your project is executed as you think. This might not be bad if that person is at least available when his or her expertise is critical. But, of course, you can never be sure this will happen.

Large research suppliers have powerful and convincing project prin-cipals and often weak and inexperienced project executors. If an inexperi-enced project executor is the person writing your questionnaire, analyzing your data and writing your recommendations, you are not getting your money's worth. As such then, is the research worth as much as you are being charged? The answer here would be unequivocally no.

If you haven't guessed, I believe that the best research comes from smaller research suppliers. These are usually companies in which the person executing your project is the person selling you the project. Often this means dealing with the company owner or a partner. In such instances, your questionnaire is being written by someone who has written hundreds or thousands of questionnaires and has analyzed data for hundreds or thousands of studies. There is simply no substitute for this kind of hands-on experience. Are those consultants worth what they charge? Unequivocally yes!

GETTING WHAT YOU'RE PAYING FOR

You get far more for your research investment when dealing with a small supplier and a highly experienced researcher. You are a very important client to a small supplier. The success of your research effort and the resulting growth of your business will provide additional opportunities that are far more meaningful to a smaller supplier than to a larger one.

Large research suppliers are far more concerned with the Krafts, P&Gs, General Foods, or Coca-Colas of the world, companies whose yearly research budgets are in the millions. For many large research suppliers, but certainly not all, a small research client is often more aggravation than opportunity. By all means, when you find a large supplier that has better capabilities to complete your project, use it. Just make sure you have experienced people working on your project.

BEING A GOOD CLIENT

You have completed your due diligence. You've found a research supplier that you trust, designed your study, negotiated a good price, and given the go-ahead to begin the project. But all that effort will be minimized if you aren't a good client. To get the most bang from your budget and from your supplier, follow the easy dos and don'ts shown in Table 6.3.

It's a two-way street. The best research suppliers have a keen interest in making your project as insightful as possible. The best clients show respect for that effort.

Table 6.3 Being a good client

Do	Don't
Pay attention to the research schedule.	Be hard to reach, be unresponsive or show little regard to the agreed-upon timelines.
Make sure others involved in the project are empowered.	Give responsibilities to others who must always check with you before a decision can be made.
Stay aware of the progress of the study.	Be a pest. The research company will inform you if there are issues that need your attention.
Expect the results when promised.	Push for faster results. It will only minimize the thinking time the supplier spends analyzing your data.
Engage people from the research supplier in a personal meeting or presentation soon after results are available.	Let the report sit around gathering dust.
Use the research supplier as part of your decision-making process.	Ignore the contribution of the supplier or consultant by not engaging him or her in how you use the research.
Pay your invoices when they are expected.	Worry the consultant about your ability to pay and make him or her bug you about overdue invoices.

7

How much research should you do?

A LITTLE CAN GO A LONG WAY

There are many ways to begin your research process. An inexpensive customer satisfaction survey or a series of focus groups is common. How far you go after that is often a function of the benefits you get from the first study. I've known clients who have milked a couple of focus groups for six months, making changes in how they approach customer service, what they say in their advertising and how their salespeople approach prospects.

In other situations, an expenditure as low as $15,000 for a survey (which is considered quite minimal) can provide information that takes a year or more to fully digest and integrate.

How far you take the results of your first study, or any study for that matter, has to do with how often you revisit the results. To maximize your research efforts, follow these guidelines:

1. *Write action plans with the results.* When you review the results of your research, write a one- or two-page action plan with dates for the completion of each action. Begin with the actions that you can immediately implement.
2. *Be disciplined.* Mark your calendar on the dates you set for each action. When the first date comes up, hopefully you will have completed that first action. If not, get going and, at the same time, revisit the research.

3. *Alter your action plan and schedule.* Time always changes your perspective on research and how you view the results. As you reread your study, some findings and recommendations will become more important and some will become less so. Every time you revisit the study you will get new insights. Actions you haven't yet taken become more or less important. You will visualize new actions and new priorities that you hadn't previously considered.
4. *Continue to follow this process.* You should continue rereading the research report for as long as it suggests new or revised actions.

Without a doubt, the biggest waste of your research expenditure is to let reports gather dust after one reading. The more attention you give every study you complete, the more your business will improve. You can take that to the bank.

AS MUCH AS EGO ALLOWS

Research reports are egoless. It's readers who suffer from an "invented here" syndrome. If you are unwilling to be objective about what your research says, if you are unwilling to be wrong about your previous decisions or if you are unwilling to test new approaches suggested by the research, you have wasted your money. You have reached the point where you know how much more research you should do. The answer is "no more."

MORE THAN YOUR COMPETITION

Of course it's hard to know the amount of research that your competitors are doing. But after you conduct your first study, you'll get an inkling. You'll likely learn things about your competitors' customers that hadn't occurred to you. It will become clear to you how and why your competitors advertise the way they do or approach their customers in a certain manner.

You will get insight into their marketing programs and better understand why they compete with you the way they do. You'll get insight into their thinking regarding pricing or why their operations or salespeople behave differently from your salespeople. Importantly, you will begin to understand why customers are your competitors' customers and not your customers.

What you may learn is that the competition has had intelligence that you're now just getting, explaining why they are stronger in the market than you – or even why they are weaker. Importantly, though, you will become armed with new information and that will allow you to compete with them far more effectively.

You could also get lucky. You might learn that your competitors are overlooking the obvious or making the same mistakes as you. You could uncover needs in the market that neither you nor your competition is addressing. Perhaps you'll see an opportunity where a small shift in emphasis could produce a unique advantage.

You will be well served to assume that your competition has the same problems as you and is probably doing research to address those problems. Without the same intelligence, you'll be at a distinct competitive disadvantage.

FOCUS ON THE LARGEST COMPETITOR

Assuming that you have your house in order and are serving your current customers well, *it is critically important to stay in tune with your largest competitor*. Big competitors should be doing everything possible to keep customers happy and loyal. But this type of competitor often becomes complacent and overlooks the obvious. It usually proves easier for you to attack the weaknesses of a big competitor and entice customers to switch than it is to outmaneuver a smaller, hungrier competitor.

Big competitors usually set the standards for both attracting and losing customers. Their marketing power may be formidable, and customers flock in their direction as a result. But being more focused on getting rather than keeping makes such competitors vulnerable to losing customers to smaller and more nimble competitors.

If you have a limited research budget, spend a portion on learning what your largest competitor is doing right and wrong. If the competition is performing better than you and you can do something about it, do it. Find the weaknesses and exploit them. Or, better yet, find a new product, benefit, or customer service approach that will delight and intrigue and at least open your door to the big competitor's customers who are ripe for the picking.

FOCUS ON SMALL COMPETITORS NEXT

It is always valuable to learn what competitors your size or smaller do to get and keep their customers. They certainly have the same problems attracting and keeping business as you do. But for whatever reasons, there are many customers who choose one of your smaller competitors rather than you to give their business to. Once you have learned how to attack your largest competitor, set your sights on your smaller ones.

Take Starbucks, for example. If you want to open a coffee shop in your neighborhood it's unlikely that you have any hope of competing directly with Starbucks. Here you'd be wise to study Joe's, Barbara's, or Pete's local coffee shop. Learn what keeps them afloat. Why do their customers keep coming back rather than going to a nearby Starbucks? Emulating or bettering their success could be the formula to success for you.

The principle is sound. Usually, markets are quite fractionated. While the big company may dominate, chances are it doesn't control more than 20 or 30 percent of the market. Find the keys to outflanking the plethora of small companies that are also your competition. Their customers might be easier for you to capture than the big competitor's.

HOW MUCH RESEARCH, REALLY

To a carpenter with a hammer, everything looks like a nail. To a researcher, every marketing problem can be solved with a research study.

In reality, there is no good answer to the question of how much research you should do. It's like trying to answer the question, "How healthy should I be?" Do you ever really get a totally clean bill of health from your doctor? Isn't there always something you could be doing to be healthier and to live longer?

It's the same with research. You can always be studying ways to grow your business. You're never really finished.

The answer probably lies somewhere between your ability to use the research information that you generate and your available funds. A client recently informed me that he wasn't going to allocate research expense for the coming year because a terrible downturn in his industry was hurting his sales, which, in turn, had made research unaffordable. He went on to say that he had received a great deal of value from his previous year's research expenditure.

I have two reactions to my client's decision. One, he was being nice to me. If he had really had value out of the money spent the previous year, he'd know that he had preserved business that would have been lost without the changes he had made to his business – changes that he wouldn't have made without benefit of the previous year's research and that it would be appropriate for him to continue.

Secondly, in a time of trouble it is always necessary to do things better and smarter. Research can help determine such directions and, in this regard, my client is being short-sighted. Even in shrinking markets, there are always opportunities. In fact, learning how to gain an advantage over struggling competitors during down periods in the market is perhaps the best time to conduct research. Ultimately, I did a lousy job of convincing my client that research should be one of the last things he should cut.

WHEN YOU RUN OUT OF QUESTIONS

Here is my top 10 list for knowing when to stop doing research. If you answer yes to any of them, buy yourself a new car, yacht, summer home, or whatever. You certainly don't need the money for research:

1. Will your business grow profitability on pure momentum?
2. Will your business grow without improvements?
3. Do you know everything that your competitors can possibly do to hinder your growth?
4. Are you convinced that you can't lose customers or gain new ones?
5. Are you convinced that there is nothing that can happen to cause your products to become obsolete?
6. Are you sure that your business isn't subject to changing trends?
7. Are you sure that you are the only one who can generate good ideas about how to run your business?
8. Are you clairvoyant?
9. Do you get tomorrow's stock market reports in today's newspaper?
10. Have you contracted for a sale of your business that will make you millions?

8

The research plan

Using Chapter 2 as a guide, you should now determine exactly what you want your research to accomplish. What do you want to learn and from whom do you want to learn it?

Your study plan should consist of three well-thought-out sections:

1. the overall study objective;
2. specific study objectives;
3. target market respondents.

THE OVERALL OBJECTIVE

The overall objective should reflect the large picture. It is usually a one- or two-sentence statement that captures the essence of what you want to learn. Below are overall objective examples from four different studies:

- *Overall objective #1 – air-conditioner study*
  "The overall objective is to determine the attributes that are important when consumers purchase window air-conditioners. Additionally, it is to determine how my company and my competitors perform relative to the things that are important."
  Stating the objective in this way focuses the study in two areas:
  - determining the areas that are important when consumers purchase air-conditioners;

- determining your company's performance in the areas that are important as against your competitors' performance in the same areas.

- *Overall objective #2 – gift box study*
"The overall objective of this research is to determine what effect, if any, a reduction in the size of the gift boxes might have on the value perceptions consumers have when contemplating purchase of a gift."
In this case, the company wishes to use less expensive, smaller boxes when packaging its gift line, which, in turn, would increase its profits. Determining the relationship of box size to box value is a precise and clear overall objective.

- *Overall objective #3 – hardware store study*
"The overall objective of this study is to determine which of three advertising approaches is most believable and would most likely draw new customers to visit the hardware store for the first time. The three approaches to be tested communicate 1) best prices, 2) best customer service, and 3) biggest variety."
The goal here is clear and concise: to generate new customers who have never been in the store before. It is also assumed that price, customer service, and variety are the strongest messages that would drive new traffic. Most importantly, believability was determined to be the criterion on which the ads would be measured.

- *Overall objective #4 – dentist study*
"The overall objective of this study is to determine the factors that are taken into consideration when choosing to change dentists – to determine the criteria that patients use when first thinking about changing dentists and whether those criteria change to ultimately cause a switch."
The objective here is general in nature. It is to better understand a decision-making process in regard to choosing a dentist. It does not suggest that a particular course of action will be taken as a result of the study findings.

By writing an overall objective statement, you are forced into determining the *big-picture goal* of your research. An associate of mine lamented about one of his clients, saying, "They always want to throw the kitchen sink into their studies. They want to learn everything there is to be learned." What my associate is rightly suggesting is that trying to focus on everything at once tends to make studies overly superficial in the areas where the in-depth information would do the most good.

If you are not clear about your overall research objective, you are more likely to create a study that collects information for the sake of the information, not for taking action. This might not be a big problem if you have the research funds necessary to study everything all at once. Usually, though, this is not a luxury that Guerrillas can afford.

SPECIFIC OBJECTIVES

Specific objectives flow from the overall objective. They provide elaboration on the overall objective and set out important areas that should be included in your survey or focus group study.

Take the example from the air-conditioner study. Here, the overall objective is: "To determine the attributes that are important when consumers purchase window air-conditioners. Additionally, it is to determine how my company and my competitors perform relative to the things that are important."

Specific objectives here would be:

1. Determine which of the following specific attributes are most important when purchasing a window air-conditioner:
    - ease of installation;
    - brand name;
    - price;
    - product warranty;
    - dealer knowledge;
    - friend or relative's recommendation;
    - cost to operate;
    - available at a nearby store.
2. Determine which of the following brands would most likely be purchased:
    - GE;
    - Frigidaire;
    - Kenmore;
    - Whirlpool;
    - Maytag.
3. Determine how the brands that would most likely be purchased rate on the attributes of importance.
4. Determine whether there are differences in how the brands are perceived by consumers who purchased window air-conditioners more than five years ago and intend to purchase a new one in the near future versus those purchasing in the past year.
5. Determine whether there are differences in perceptions based on the area of the country where consumers live.

The specific objectives lay out the attributes that will be measured as well as specific brands to be compared. They also state that the study should collect information among recent air-conditioner purchasers as against those intending to purchase in the near future. It is also to understand geographic differences that might exist.

Take the overall objective of the gift box study: "The overall objective of this research is to determine what effect, if any, a reduction in the size of the gift boxes might have on the value perceptions consumers have when contemplating purchase of a gift."

In this study, the specific objectives are:

1. What is the overall purchase interest in the large boxed gifts versus the smaller boxed gifts? Does "intent to purchase" deteriorate because the gifts come packaged in smaller boxes?
2. In comparison to the larger boxed gifts, are two different sizes of smaller boxed gifts perceived as better, worse, or the same in terms of:
   - being a gift of good value;
   - being a gift of good quality;
   - being a gift that the giver would be proud to give;
   - being a gift that is pleasing to look at in the box;
   - being a gift that when gift-wrapped might be one that appears intriguing and be among the first to be opened?
3. Which of three graphic approaches for smaller boxed gifts is better at communicating value, quality, and the other attributes?
4. Would consumers who have not purchased boxed gifts be more or less likely to purchase if the box size were reduced?

Stating the specific objectives in this precise manner lays out all the factors by which the small and large boxes will be measured. In doing so, it provides a variety of data on which to base a final decision.

Assume that overall purchase intent as stated in objective 1 does not produce decisive information as to a winning box. The additional information that will now be gathered for objectives 2, 3, and 4 could be used to break a tie. If purchase intent is equal but the smaller boxes outperform the larger ones on the other issues, there is added information for making a decision. Further, if it is determined that the smaller boxes do not reduce the number of new buyers attracted to the gift products, the decision becomes even easier.

Now take a last example from the dentist study: 'The overall objective of this study is to determine the factors that are taken into consideration when choosing to change dentists – to determine the criteria that patients use when first thinking about changing dentists and whether those criteria change to ultimately cause a switch."

Specific objectives would be as follows:

1. What are all the considerations present when a patient first contemplates changing dentists?
2. Do those considerations change in any way while contemplating a change?
3. Do new considerations become important in the period leading up to a change?
4. Do patients express dissatisfaction to their dentist prior to changing? Why, or why not? If considerations are expressed, what is the reaction of the dentist?
5. Do patients interview one or more new dentists prior to changing? If so, what is said by the patient, and the potential dentist, regarding a change?
6. When the change is actually made, did the dentist being terminated make the change difficult or uncomfortable?

The specific objectives in this study are considered *exploratory* in nature. They lay out a broad range of issues that the research seeks to explore. They do not assume certain factors or problems exist around which questioning must revolve. Rather, the research is intended to shed light on the process and to surface factors that might be important when changing dentists.

TARGET MARKET RESPONDENTS

Every market research study has *target market respondents*. These are the respondents whose opinions are deemed to be most important. Target market respondents can have a multitude of characteristics. They can:

- have particular demographic characteristics (e.g., be single or married, have large families or small families, be college graduates or have only a high school education, have incomes under or over a specified amount per year, etc.);
- use particular products or brands;
- purchase only from you, only from your competitors, or from both of you;
- be customers who purchased from you once or who purchased many times;
- be customers who bought a great deal from you in the past but are no longer buying.

The possible customers and prospects that you could target in a research study can be wide and varied. Therefore, in planning your research it is usually necessary to *set priorities* and to *narrow the respondent target field*.

Consider the following target market scenarios:

- If you are conducting a poll to determine who voters will vote for in an upcoming election, your target market might be as general as registered voters.
- If you want to grow sales quickly, you might want to interview your customers who are also purchasing from a competitor. The goal here would be a very precise target, and the objective would be to learn how to convince your customers to give their additional expenditure to you instead of a competitor.
- If you are striving to convert prospects who have never purchased the kinds of products you sell, you might want to target respondents who have never purchased from you but have demographic characteristics that are comparable to those of your current customers.
- If you are seeking to develop and sell new products or services, you might want to target respondents who are unusually imaginative and more likely to give you good ideas.
- If you want to sell more from your catalog, your target respondents might be people who requested your catalog but have not yet purchased from it.

There are a number of questions you should ask yourself in determining your target market:

1. What targets offer you the best opportunity of increasing your business the fastest?
2. What targets would be important for longer-term growth?
3. What targets would be least costly to convince to buy more from you?
4. What targets would provide nice information to know but would be too costly to attract?
5. If you knew the attitudes of one particular target, could you extrapolate to other targets without having to study them?
6. Do you have the research budget available to cast a very wide net? By collecting data across many targets at the same time, you could then determine which are easiest to sell to once you see the data.

The study plan is a dynamic tool. It serves to focus your initial thinking, and it also serves as a discussion document. No doubt others in your company have opinions regarding your objectives and targets. Certainly your vendors, particularly your ad agency, sales promotion or public relations company could provide advice. The study plan helps everyone focus their thinking.

Developing a study plan eliminates guessing. It provides a framework for everyone to agree on the important areas to study. It also gives life to the fact that research is important and, if approached from the right angle, will help grow your business. And, as you will see in later chapters, it will prove critical in choosing the right methodology for conducting the research.

Use the following to develop your final study plan:

1. State your overall research objective:

2. State your secondary research objectives:
    a.

    b.

    c.

    d.

    e.

3. Describe in as much detail as possible the target markets you wish to research:
    – Target #1:

    – Target #2:

    – Target #3:

4. Research methodology (once you have read Chapters 9 and 11, on focus groups and surveys respectively, you will be able to complete the research methodology):

9

Focus groups

WHAT ARE THEY REALLY?

When most people think of market research, they think about focus groups. How many times in an election year have you heard "Well, our focus groups told us that it's about the economy"? Or "We conducted focus groups, and people really liked the new flavor"? Or "Our focus groups said that this was really a product that women would like more than men"?

While focus groups are universally known, they are also universally misunderstood. As I discussed in Chapter 3, focus groups are a qualitative tool. The word "qualitative" means "observational." "Observation" means:

- becoming aware of patterns of thinking that exist;
- becoming aware of images and perceptions;
- learning the range of likes and dislikes that exist;
- hearing suggestions and ideas;
- hearing arguments for and against;
- hearing stories good and bad;
- discovering notions positive and negative.

When observing issues, no value whatsoever should be placed on whether one issue is more important than another. You cannot know if an issue is true for one person or a million people. *You cannot do anything more than know that the issue exists.*

Is it important to know that issues exist? Of course, but it's only a first step. To place reliance on opinions and ideas expressed in focus groups can be marketing and financial suicide. *In fact, if you plan on making a major decision from focus groups alone, you should probably save your money and make an educated guess.*

How, then, should focus groups be used? They should be used:

1. *To create a platform or context.* Focus groups are a first step. They are exploratory in nature, with the sole purpose of viewing the options around the issue, "getting a handle" on the factors that might be influential, and understanding better the conditions that exist in the minds of customers and prospects.
2. *To clarify thinking and to set objectives.* Focus groups seek to clarify thinking around the problem so that precise research objectives can be set. They allow you to gauge what you don't know and should seek to learn.
3. *To determine the right questions.* Focus groups help to determine the questions to ask and how to ask them.
4. *To provide an indication of where opportunities exist.* Focus groups show what seems to be working or not working. They point to areas where improvements or changes might be indicated or where unmet wants, needs, wishes, and desires might exist.
5. *To examine possibilities.* Focus groups allow us to ask "What if?" What if we did more or less of that – might our business increase? What new things could be tried that might work to give us a competitive advantage or to increase the odds for success?

The value of focus groups lies in discovering what's going on, but not whether you should do anything about it.

SETTING FOCUS GROUP OBJECTIVES AND A DISCUSSION GUIDE

Below are the objectives of a typical focus group study, in this case for a wallpaper catalog of the Apex Company.

The overall objectives are twofold: 1) to gain an understanding of attitudes that consumers have toward purchasing from wallpaper catalogs received in the mail; and 2) to further explore attitudes toward improving catalogs so that consumers would be more likely to purchase from them.

Specific objectives regarding the catalogs include:

- determining the elements that cause consumers to open and inspect the wallpaper catalogs that arrive in their homes;

- determining the attitudes consumers have toward large 80-page catalogs versus smaller 40-page catalogs;
- determining the strengths and weaknesses of a number of catalogs not competing in the marketplace;
- identifying areas that might be addressed for the Apex catalog so that it becomes the desired source for purchasing wallpaper.

As is evident, the objectives here are not to determine what is most or least important to consumers when purchasing from wallpaper catalogs. They are simply *to determine the range of issues* that is part of the decision-making process. This is the proper use of focus groups.

The discussion guide below addresses the research objectives and could be used when conducting the focus groups:

1. *Background:*
   - introductions, etc.;
   - likes/dislikes in purchasing wallpaper from catalogs;
   - whether recently purchased/considering purchase of wallpaper;
   - factors in determining whether to purchase from a catalog versus going to a retail store.
2. *Catalogs:*
   - When wallpaper catalogs arrive in your home, what catches your attention? What makes you decide to look at some catalogs and not others?
   - What is it about the cover that grabs your attention? What is it about some catalogs that causes you to look through them, while others are just glanced at?

   Probe importance:
   - of a well-recognized name in the decision to inspect a wallpaper catalog when it arrives;
   - of products being new, unique, and different from what might have been seen elsewhere;
   - of price, clear descriptions;
   - of companies that have their own credit plans in addition to normal credit cards;
   - of being able to track the status of order by phone or online.
3. *Catalog companies:*
   - Which wallpaper catalog companies are you aware of? Which companies have you purchased from? Why those?
   - Which wallpaper catalog companies are you aware of but have not purchased from? Why those? What causes some to be purchased from but not others?

- List catalogs purchased from/aware of. Compare how they differ in terms of:
  - quality of merchandise;
  - ease of shopping;
  - offering good prices/good promotions;
  - customer service;
  - reputation;
  - price.

4. *Apex versus competition:*
   - Pass out two Apex and two competitors' catalogs. Allow respondents 15 minutes to review. Have respondents make notes as to what they liked/disliked about each catalog.
   - Rank the catalogs in terms of most to least compelling. Which catalog did you find most compelling? [Choose the most compelling.] Why that one? List the areas liked/disliked.

   Probe:
   - Does the catalog allow making a buying decision easy?
   - In what ways is the catalog helpful?
   - Is the catalog easy to read? In what ways?
   - Is the catalog unique/different from the others? In what ways?
   - How do you feel about the manner in which the products are shown and described? What about the quality of the photographs/product colors being true?
   - What about the merchandised categories/depth and breadth of selection?
   - What about the prices?
   - If you want to place an order, could you do so without calling the number given for help? If not, what would you need to know?
   - What additional information would you need to make a decision to purchase from the catalog?

   Repeat the above process for the other three catalogs.

It should be clear from the discussion guide that this focus group study is to obtain background learning and generate ideas as to what the Apex catalog could do to be more competitive. *At no time do the objectives or the discussion guide attempt to develop a consensus or determine issues that are most important.*

The results of these focus groups allow the company to develop a list of areas that could be addressed to make the catalog more competitive. This list could then be researched through a second research *survey* designed to determine which ones would provide the greatest competitive advantage.

WHAT SHOULD I EXPECT FROM FOCUS GROUPS?

At the completion of a focus group study, you should be smarter about your problem. You should have a better understanding of where you might "focus" your products, company, marketing, or advertising to be more successful. As a result, you will have uncovered options that you should consider to help grow your business.

But no matter how compelling the findings from focus groups are, you should resist the temptation to jump into costly action. Don't let yourself be lured into making decisions because 30 or 40 people had a certain opinion. Worse yet, don't get big-headed because most of the focus group respondents agree with your thinking or pet theories on an issue. Don't think you have finished your research. *Rather, realize that now you better understand the issues and the potential solutions and can begin to determine the ones that will make you the most money.*

SETTING UP FOCUS GROUPS

There is a variety of things to consider when planning focus groups: the composition of the groups, how many groups, whether certain locations are better than others, and whether a male or female moderator might be more appropriate.

The question of male versus female moderator is an interesting issue. Years ago, I had a pharmaceutical client that marketed birth control pills. All its focus groups had been conducted among female respondents by a female moderator, which seemed fitting. The company liked the way I moderated focus groups for its headache products and asked me if I'd be willing to moderate a couple of birth control focus groups among women – just to experiment. The rationale was that, my being a male moderator, I could play dumb and the women would tell me things that they might think would be obvious to a female moderator and therefore not express. I reluctantly agreed to conduct the groups.

The groups were uncomfortable for me and difficult for the women. I found myself blushing and embarrassed when asking the women highly personal questions about their sex lives. The women were squirming in their chairs and reluctant to give me more than curt answers. At the end of each group, I told the women we were experimenting and asked them how they felt about having a male as a moderator. The answer I remember most came from a beautiful 25-year-old single woman who said, "Well, you were very professional, but you just don't get it. Men wouldn't."

Most of the time, though, it really doesn't matter whether the moderator is male or female. A competent moderator can effectively address the objectives of any discussion guide. If you have a particularly sensitive topic, just use your common sense in deciding whether a male or female moderator is more appropriate to ask the questions. When planning focus groups, also consider the following points.

Keep the respondents as homogeneous as possible

Once you have developed your research objectives, you must determine the customer or prospect targets who would provide you with the greatest opportunity for growth. Do you want to persuade heavy users to spend even more? Light users to become heavy? Users of your competitors' products to become users of your products? Do you want to attract younger customers, higher-income customers, or men more than women?

Set priorities. Don't try to learn everything about everybody all at once. When you conduct groups among respondents who have similar perspectives, it is far easier to crystallize a perspective about that target.

When you mix targets in the same group, it's more difficult to determine whether answers that come from one target influence the answers from another. You may fail to get consistent points of view because you have such different respondent lifestyles and demographics, and this can get in the way of clear learning.

There are certainly times when it might be productive to mix respondent types: mixing perhaps older and younger respondents, men and women, or heavy users and light users. Doing this will generate a wide and disjointed range of attitudes, perspectives, opinions, and preferences, which might be the best thing to do, given your focus group goals. Just realize that, when you interview disparate targets at the same time, it is more difficult to develop cohesive theories about any one target.

Always conduct more than one group of a type

If you decide that you want to understand attitudes of heavy and light users better, conduct two groups for each type. If you want to focus on the attitudes of younger as against older respondents, conduct two groups for each. Remember, it is always prudent to conduct two groups for each type rather than rely on the attitudes of one group.

This truism comes from the fact that, even though respondents have similar characteristics, it doesn't mean they will have the same attitudes and perceptions. In fact, you should expect to hear diametrically opposed attitudes from a first group to a second group. The trick, in fact, is in trying to figure out why respondents who have similar characteristics have such different opinions.

You'll also find that a first group provides the broad strokes. It allows you to begin to understand attitudes and productive lines of questioning. By then following the most productive lines of questioning in a second group, your learning builds dramatically. Taking the two together, you develop a richer understanding and appreciation of the issues that exist.

As moderators like to say, "Conducting only one group for a particular target can be idiosyncratic." Therefore, always conduct two of a type to ensure that your first wasn't a bunch of eccentric or peculiar respondents.

Consider multiple locations

Assuming you do business in more than one area, consider at least two geographic locations for your focus groups. Because attitudes and perceptions often differ geographically, it is prudent to represent at least two areas. If you sense that attitudes differ, you'd have to consider different marketing approaches based on geographic differences.

FOCUS GROUP FACILITIES

There are focus group facilities available for moderators to rent in almost every major market. These facilities exist for the sole purpose of supporting moderators wishing to conduct focus groups. If you need a moderator, most will provide one (for a fee, of course) or refer you to moderators whom they have worked with. The facilities provide a range of services that include:

- renting discussion rooms that allow clients to observe the groups without being seen by respondents;
- recruiting the types of respondents you want in your groups and making sure they show up when they are scheduled;
- providing specialized respondent recruiting such as medical doctors, business executives, people with certain medical conditions, high-tech respondents, children, older people, ethnic respondents, etc.;
- handling the incentives (usually money) that respondents receive for attending the groups;

- providing test kitchens;
- providing audiotaping, videotaping, and other audio and video equipment that you might need;
- ordering and serving refreshments or meals.

Working with focus group facilities is very easy. A person is assigned to your project who will work with you on costs and then make sure that all aspects of your focus group study proceed smoothly.

Finding a group facility is also simple. There is a directory called *Impulse Survey of Focus Facilities* that is published every year. The directory lists hundreds of focus group facilities throughout the United States as well as internationally. Each facility is rated by the moderators who have used the facility in the past. An overall rating is provided, as are individual ratings regarding the quality of recruiting, staff, the facility itself, location, food, and value.

You can browse through a number of facilities in an area and call the ones that are convenient or have the highest ratings. I usually find myself calling the ones that provide a toll-free number.

The cost of the directory is $80 per year in the United States, and you can get it by phone (310–559–6892), fax (310–839–9770), e-mail (info@impulsesurvey.com) or internet (www.impulsesurvey.com). You can also check out www.quirks.com and www.bluebook.org for a free listing of focus group facilities.

FACILITY COSTS

Focus group facilities provide cost estimates for each of the services that it provides. Costs are broken down as follows:

1. *Room rental.* You can expect a cost of $400 to $500 for a typical two-hour focus group. Multiply this by the number of groups you will be conducting. The cost includes the focus group conference room, an easel for writing, pens and paper for the respondents, and audiotaping of the group. It also includes the cost of the observation room, where 6 to 12 people can sit comfortably and watch the group unobserved, as well as a host or hostess to make sure everything runs smoothly.
2. *Recruiting.* This cost is variable and can range from a low of about $70 per respondent to a high of $200 per respondent. Average cost is about $90. This means that, if you are recruiting 10 people to attend your group, you simply multiply your cost for recruiting that group by 10. If

you are conducting four groups, you then multiply by 4. Recruiting costs can vary by how easy or difficult the facilities feel it will be to find types of respondents that you want for your groups (see the next section on focus group screeners). Most focus group facilities have a database of people who have indicated a willingness to attend groups, and the majority of group studies use respondents who are screened and recruited from these databases. The facilities can also recruit respondents from lists that you might provide. Perhaps you wish to conduct groups among your customers and have customer names, phone numbers, and zip codes available. Or, depending on your precise need, facilities can recruit respondents using local phone directories or by placing small ads in local newspapers.

3. *Incentives.* It is customary for respondents to be paid a monetary incentive for attending groups. Incentives are generally in the same range as recruiting costs. If it costs $70 per recruit, a $70 incentive usually will suffice. If the cost is $200 per recruit, the incentive will be in the $200 range. If you recruit 40 respondents for four groups with a $70 incentive, you could end up paying out $2,800 if all 40 respondents actually show up for the group. Usually two to four respondents per group will fail to show, and you will not be charged incentives for the no-show respondents. Occasionally, other incentives are used (e.g., products, coupons, big discounts when purchasing from certain stores, etc.) but these are usually less effective in motivating respondents to participate and ensuring that they actually show up.

4. *Other costs.* There are other variable costs that will be itemized in the estimate a facility provides. These include food and refreshments that you order. Some facilities include free videotaping as part of the room rental fee but not too many, and special audio and video equipment such as projectors, computers, etc. are often needed and will cost extra. Many facilities also have a full kitchen available if your study calls for special food preparation.

FOCUS GROUP SCREENERS

A focus group screener is a short questionnaire moderators provide to the focus group facility, which is used to screen the respondents. Below is an example of a typical screener for a camera store wishing to conduct focus groups about digital cameras. Note the explanation of the various sections of the screener.

Digital camera screener

Hello, my name is _____ from _____, a market research firm. I want to assure you that this is not a sales call. We are conducting a study among people concerning the purchase of cameras. May I have a few minutes of your time? Good.

1. First of all, are you, or is any member of your household, employed in the camera industry, such as manufacturers, distributors, or retailers of cameras? IF YES, TERMINATE.

   Explanation: It is usually desirable to screen out respondents who work in or are associated with the industry in which your focus groups are being conducted. This is done to ensure that atypical respondents do not participate in the groups or that a potential competitor does not sneak in and become aware of your research.

2. In the past six months, have you participated in any research studies or focus groups conducted for any company selling cameras? IF YES, TERMINATE.

   Explanation: It is unwise to allow respondents into a group if they have had recent experience in the research topic, as they tend to become overly informed about the topic and therefore would be considered atypical. There are some cases, though, where familiarity with a topic is helpful and provides valuable input. In such a case, this screening question would be eliminated. The advisability of recruiting such respondents will be discussed later in this chapter.

3. When it comes to buying cameras for you or your family, are you the primary decision maker as to where a purchase would be made? IF NO, ASK TO SPEAK TO THAT PERSON.

   Explanation: You want to speak immediately to the person whom you want to participate in your group. There is no point in screening a respondent only to find out later that the person is not the decision maker when it comes to your products or services.

4. Do you have children of school age living at home? IF NO, TERMINATE.
5. Do you have a computer in your home? IF NO, TERMINATE.
6. Do you personally use a cell phone, pager, PDA or laptop computer on a regular basis? IF NO, TERMINATE.
7. How interested are you in digital cameras and digital photography? Are you:

    – Very interested   _____
    – Somewhat interested   _____
    – Not interested   _____
RECRUIT AS MANY AS POSSIBLE WHO ARE VERY OR SOMEWHAT
INTERESTED.

*Explanation: This series of questions is intended to leave only respon-
dents who have children living in their home and are technologically
savvy. As you will surmise from the screening questions that follow, the
goal of this group is to explore attitudes toward the purchase of digital
cameras. These questions will ensure that respondents are in the
desired target.*

    *Of course, you would have to decide what questions would be
appropriate to ask when recruiting for your particular study.*

8. In the past 120 days have you personally gone to a retail store and
   shopped for or purchased a camera? IF NO, TERMINATE.

*Explanation: Since the company selling digital cameras is a retailer, it is
important to ensure that respondents coming into the group have
personally shopped at retail stores in the recent past and not just made
a decision to purchase using the internet or a catalog.*

    *If appropriate, you would use a question like this to qualify respon-
dents for your groups.*

9. What one retail store that sells cameras do you shop at most often?
   Do not read list. RECRUIT A GOOD MIX OF STORES.
       – Target   _____
       – Wal-Mart   _____
       – Costco   _____
       – Other   _____
       IF OTHER, TERMINATE.

*Explanation: In this case, the focus group is to be conducted among a
mix of customers loyal to the above three stores. If the study was being
conducted for Wal-Mart and they wished to identify Target customers
for their groups, this question would be appropriate. The same
question could be used to identify and recruit those loyal to any other
competitor. A similar question could be used if you are trying to recruit
your customers for the groups.*

10. Approximately what percentage of your technology purchases for
    your household-products such as cameras, computers, PDAs, or
    entertainment products – are made:

    – At a retail store   _____
      MUST BE AT LEAST 51 PERCENT.
    – Using a catalog and phone or fax   _____
    – Using the internet   _____

Explanation: The study is designed to determine attitudes toward purchasing digital cameras from retail stores. Again, it is important here to recruit shoppers whose primary channel of purchase is a retail store rather than another channel.

We would like to invite you to attend a focus group discussion about purchasing digital cameras. The session will be held on [date] at [time]. The location of the group is [address]. You will be paid for your participation.

    Prior to the focus group we would like you to visit a retail store near you. We would ask you to look around the digital camera department and fill out a brief questionnaire. And, again, I want to reiterate that no one will attempt to sell you anything as a result of your participation. Are you willing to attend? Good.

Explanation: Prior to attending the focus group, respondents are being asked to visit the digital camera department of a retail store. Therefore, the experience will be fresh in their minds when they attend the group, and they will be better able to express their attitudes and opinions regarding how digital cameras are being sold.

    As previously pointed out, it is sometimes helpful to have respondents become more informed about the topic before they attend groups. Shopping assignments are a good way to accomplish this.

    I just have a few more questions for classification purposes.
11. Is your age (RECRUIT A GOOD MIX):
    – Under 21   _____
    – 21 to 34   _____
    – 35 to 44   _____
    – 45 to 54   _____
    – 55 or over   _____
12. Are you employed (RECRUIT A GOOD MIX):
    – Full time   _____
    – Part time   _____
    – Not employed   _____
13. Is your total family income before taxes:
    – Under $50,000   _____

DO NOT RECRUIT MORE THAN 3 RESPONDENTS.
– Over $50,000 _____

Explanation: There are usually a number of demographic questions that are part of a screener. Setting demographic quotas ensures that the group is not made up of respondents who have the same characteristics. In this case, age, employment status, and income are important for ensuring a good mix.

Please mark your calendar for [repeat date and time]. Do you want us to mail you the questionnaire or fax it? If fax, what is your fax number?

We will call you in several days to make sure you received the questionnaire and also to remind you of the time of the focus group. If for some reason you cannot attend, will you please call us at [number] and let us know? Thank you.

Name

Address

Phone

Explanation: It is always wise to follow up with respondents to ensure that they received what might be needed for the group and to remind them to attend.

Focus group screeners can be relatively simple and straightforward or quite complex. Questioning should be precise enough to ensure that you are recruiting respondents whose opinions are representative of your target. Clearly, you want to avoid spending a great deal of money recruiting respondents who are not the ones you should have questioned. Whatever the number of questions it takes to accomplish this task will determine the length of your screener.

Of course, there are times when, no matter how hard you try, your screener fails to ask the exact questions that are necessary to identify the right target. In such cases, ending up with a few wrong respondents can be a learning experience anyway. At the least you'll then have information that will cause you to question your target market assumptions and be better able to develop the necessary screening questions the next time around.

HOW TO BE AN EFFECTIVE FOCUS GROUP MODERATOR

Should you be moderating your focus groups or should you pay an experienced moderator to conduct your groups? That's like asking lawyers if they should represent themselves in a criminal trial, with common wisdom saying they'd have fools for clients. Nevertheless, there are many lawyers who can, and do, argue their own cases and are quite successful at it.

If you're going to be an effective moderator, you have to start sometime. And if you have what it takes, it won't be long before you're pretty good. To decide if moderating is for you, consider the following necessities.

Suspend your ego

Good moderators have no ego involved in the topic. They don't care if respondents like something or not. They aren't interested in convincing anybody of anything. They have absolutely no position on the subject. They are neutral and allow everyone's ideas to be equally valid. They are there to learn and to ensure that everyone is heard. *They are totally unbiased.*

This is arguably the most important aspect in moderating successful focus groups. I have seen company presidents, marketing directors, brand managers, and market research people attempt to moderate. These are very smart people who know a lot about their products and services, certainly far more than the respondents in their focus groups. But they are disasters when it comes to being effective moderators.

The minute a group gets an inkling that the moderator has a position on the subject, that group is lost. Nothing will turn off a group faster than a moderator who doesn't know how to phrase questions in an unbiased manner. A moderator who seemingly invalidates a respondent's opinion because of a need either to prove the respondent wrong or to change the respondent's point of view to that of the moderator will lose that respondent totally – and most likely everyone else in the group.

To determine if you can suspend your ego when conducting focus groups, give an honest answer to the following questions:

- Can you be totally unbiased for two hours?
- Can you refrain from being defensive?
- Can you smile at respondents when you are seething inside because you don't like what you hear?

- Can you let the respondents be the experts that they pretend to be even if they haven't a clue what they're talking about?
- Can you learn how to phrase questions so that respondents have the space to change an opinion but not feel intimidated or diminished in doing so?
- Can you suspend judgment regarding silly, stupid, uninformed, or misinformed respondents?
- Can you regard every opinion as equally valid whether you like the respondent or not, or whether he or she is a pain in the neck or not?
- Can you seem relaxed and not be flustered when you get off track or hear something that suddenly throws you off?
- Can you listen effectively to respondents whom you might regard as below your social status?
- Can you suspend your vested interest in what the focus group is telling you?
- Can you refrain from being frustrated and confused when one group after another is telling you a different story or giving you a different picture?

If you answer NO to any of these questions, consider hiring a professional moderator and studying his or her skills until you feel comfortable with your ego issues. Otherwise you'll be wasting your money trying to moderate your own groups.

Be relaxed

The first few years I moderated, I would perspire in groups. I was nervous. I worried about everything. What was the client observing my groups thinking? Was I going to be able to get around to all the questions on my discussion guide? Were the respondents saying things I thought my client wanted to hear? Was I asking questions the right way and in the right tone? I was not a relaxed moderator.

In and of itself, being on edge needn't hinder your ability to conduct an effective focus group. I was a great moderator in those days even though I was very nervous going into a new study. But it didn't hinder my ability to suspend my ego and trust where I was going. And it didn't compromise my ability to listen effectively to my respondents.

As I gained more experience moderating, I learned to relax and enjoy the time I had with each group. Two-hour groups went by in a flash. I became sharp in my ability to maintain a broad perspective when large strategic issues were being explored. And when close-in tactical issues were the focus, I became adept at exploring the minutiae of a topic.

If you can suspend your ego and learn to relax when moderating, you can become a good moderator. The rest is simply practice. Read on.

Be aware of where you're going

One focus group is never the same as the next. If your focus group study calls for four groups, you can be assured that each group will be different from the previous one – sometimes subtly so, sometimes radically so.

Many moderators, both new and experienced, become confused when respondents who are recruited to have the same characteristics, say your best customers, express totally divergent points of view. In the first group, the best customers might talk glowingly about product quality, while in the second they might focus on great service and make little mention of product quality. The third and fourth group could be a bunch of complainers regarding product quality and service – even though they are great customers.

Remember, focus groups are not about achieving consensus

Just as you are beginning to find a consistent pattern in what focus group respondents are saying, and just as you are becoming comfortable thinking you have a handle on the problem, things are likely to change. All your theories will go down the drain. And, believe me, you will find yourself flustered and lost.

What is critical to remember is that a focus group study should be viewed in its entirety – and in retrospect. Just as you should suspend your ego when moderating, you should suspend judgment about what you are hearing until after all the groups have been completed. If the study calls for four two-hour focus groups, you will have an eight-hour continuum of discussion.

What takes place in the first hour is no more or less valid or important than what takes place in the last hour. *The goal is to observe a range of thinking and range of attitudes and then begin to analyze what you have heard.*

Don't become frustrated because you can't achieve consensus. In fact, "consensus" is not a word that applies to focus groups. But be aware of where you are going, and remember that being aware means knowing that:

- all the groups should be *completed* before you reflect totally on what you hear;
- ideas, thoughts, and thinking patterns as expressed in one group should be *explored* in the next and, if you fail to receive consistent responses, the goal is to understand why this is happening;

- *exploring* why you are getting negative opinions in one group but positive opinions in another is what groups are about;
- focus groups are never about achieving closure, but rather about observing the options;
- the more *disparate* the opinions and attitudes, the better the job you are doing as a moderator.

Seasoned moderators enjoy a certain lack of consistency in their focus group studies. In instances when groups concur on an issue, there is the strong temptation for any moderator to think that the results will hold true for everyone – that they are projectable. It's easy to be duped into a false sense of security.

Remember, survey research is the only way to determine whether the different opinions and ideas expressed in focus groups are important or unimportant and to determine which ones are the keys to improving your business.

THE WARM-UP

Respondents in focus groups don't know each other, and they certainly don't know you. As the moderator, it's your job to put people at ease immediately and to let them know that what they have to say is important. To accomplish this in less than 10 or 15 minutes, try these techniques for warming up a group:

- *The standard moderator approach.* Most moderators go around the table and have respondents introduce themselves one at a time. Typically it goes something like: "Hi, I'm Bob. I've been conducting focus groups for a number of years. I'm an independent moderator and I'm hired to talk to people on many different topics. I want you to know that there are no right or wrong answers here. I'm just interested in your opinions, no matter what they might be. I'd like to first go around the room and have everyone introduce themselves. Susan, let's start with you. Tell me a little about yourself. Where do you live? Do you have a family? If you work, what type of work do you do?" The moderator then continues around the table, referring to the name card in front of each respondent and addressing each by name.
- *The inclusion approach.* Using this approach, you would introduce yourself as suggested above. But rather than going around the room one at a time, you would say to the group: "In a minute I want you to

turn to the person next to you and introduce yourself. I'd like you to find out a little bit about that person such as if they have a family, the type of work they do, whether they've had a good or bad day. Then I'm going to ask you to introduce that person to the rest of the group. OK. John, say hello to Susan. Bill, say hello to Jack [and so on]." After pairing off respondents, the moderator leaves the room for a few minutes while the respondents talk to each other. I like the inclusion approach because it immediately connects one respondent with another, forming a bond. It gives respondents the feeling that they're not alone. Most importantly, it raises the energy level in the room because everyone is engaged at once. After a few minutes of chatter, the moderator returns and asks for everyone's attention. Respondents should be told to talk one at a time because it's difficult for the moderator to follow what one person is saying when there are side conversations or when people interrupt each other. The moderator then turns to the first pair and says, "John, tell me about Susan."

- *The jump-right-into-it approach.* Often a good way to start a focus group is to immediately tell respondents about the topic. For example, the moderator could say, "We're going to talk today about shopping for a new car. What I'd like to have each of you do is take a pencil and paper and write down what you like about shopping for a new car and what you dislike." After giving respondents a few minutes to write, the moderator asks respondents to introduce themselves and then read their likes or dislikes about new car shopping. The moderator could also have respondents say hello to each other per the inclusion approach and have them create a list of likes and dislikes together.

The approach you use often depends on the topic and the types of respondents in the group. Professional groups (medical doctors, lawyers, and business executives) are not particularly comfortable with the inclusion approach. They often feel silly introducing a stranger in these circumstances. And tradespeople or blue-collar respondents are often ill at ease when asked to introduce someone they have just met. For most other types of respondents, though, the inclusion technique is a good approach for making people feel comfortable and putting them in the mood to talk.

Here are a couple of other hints to make people feel comfortable during the warm-up:

- Don't be too serious. Smile. Chuckle when a chuckle is appropriate.
- Share a little of yourself as long as it reveals nothing about your opinions on the topic. Tell a respondent, "I know how you feel when kids scream in restaurants. That happens to me a lot."

- Stroll around the room while people are introducing themselves. It breaks the formality of the situation.
- Dress casually. Respondents relate better to a casually dressed moderator than to one who is stiff and formally dressed.

ALWAYS CALL ON PEOPLE BY NAME

Some moderators are great at remembering names. If you are so blessed, refrain from using respondent name cards on the conference table. Just introduce yourself as respondents come into the room, and get their names in return. You'll find that respondents love the fact that you remembered their name and tend to be more open in their remarks as a result.

Most moderators don't want to work that hard at remembering names and prefer to use name cards. No problem. But, whether you remember names or use name cards, addressing respondents by their names is very important.

In every group, there will be some respondents who will be more aggressive than others in giving their opinions. The bane of any moderator's existence is having one or two overly verbal, overly opinionated respondents in a group. Such respondents will dominate a group if the moderator lets them.

When a question is posed to the group in general, the respondents likely to offer their opinions first will be the verbal ones. For example, the moderator might say, "I'd like to talk about what it's like to open a new checking account at a bank. What are your thoughts?" If the moderator continues to ask questions of the group in general, the same two, three, or four people will be the ones who pipe up. The better approach is "I'd like to talk about what it's like to open a new checking account at a bank. What are your thoughts, John?"

Just because a respondent must be coaxed to respond to a question does not make his or her opinions any more or less valid than those of a dominant respondent. As a moderator, you must be constantly aware of the *equal-time rule*. At the conclusion of the group, you should be clear as to where each and every respondent is coming from on virtually each and every question. If you find that you can only recall the opinions of a few, you have not obeyed the equal-time rule. You have let the few dominate the many.

Directing questions to respondents by name not only makes the laid-back respondents feel that their opinions are as valid as anyone's, but it sends a message to overbearing respondents by quieting them down. Most importantly, though, it evens out the discussion and allows the moderator to understand each respondent's unique perspective.

LISTEN INTENTLY

Good moderators have an ability to pick up nuances and details that make for immensely productive groups. They are able to focus their complete attention on the respondent doing the talking. They can blank out all the other noise going on in their mind.

When one respondent is talking, there is a strong tendency for moderators to think about the next question or the next respondent they should call upon. I will tell you that it's impossible to listen carefully while thinking too far ahead. If you are overly concerned with where to go next, you will not be likely to seize on a thought-provoking comment that could trigger an extremely productive line of questioning.

Yet being able to listen intently to one respondent while thinking two questions ahead is also important in being an effective moderator. Some moderators have a natural ability in this regard; others just never get it. To get better at listening, follow these guidelines:

- *Paraphrase.* This means picking up on what one respondent says and using it to address another. Susan makes the comment, "I love it when my husband buys my clothes. He has a great knack for picking up on the next big trend." The comment implies that Susan likes trendy clothes but may not trust her own judgment to choose new styles. Paraphrase the thought by turning to Hilary and saying, "I hear Susan saying she likes trendy clothes and really trusts her husband to make choices for her. How do you feel about that, Hilary?" Paraphrasing is one of the techniques that will cause moderators to listen more intently.
- *Write it down.* As respondents are talking and making points, moderators can scribble notes to themselves. I like standing at an easel and making notes right in front of the group. In addition to forcing me to listen carefully, it also makes respondents feel that what they are saying is important. Other moderators prefer to make notes on a pad while sitting at the conference table. A combination of both also works well. While making notes, put an innocuous mark (*, !, ^) next to comments that you feel are interesting and deserve further probing or paraphrasing. By writing down respondent comments at various times throughout the group, you'll find yourself worrying less about remembering everything being said and more about the tone, manner, and substance in which respondents express themselves. This will give you the space to focus on comments as they're being made.
- *Recap.* Recapping is a cousin to paraphrasing, but broader in scope. Assume you've just finished questioning mothers about the challenges

of raising children. You have your notes and you take 30 seconds to look them over. You might recap by saying, "OK, you gave me a lot of issues. They include academic concerns, social concerns, and concerns about being well-rounded and having outside hobbies and activities." You could then turn to Emily and say, "Emily, how would you recap what everyone has said?" Recapping gives everyone a second chance to express themselves. It forces respondents to express in their own words what they've heard. By doing so, you'll find new and different takes on the subject.

- *Moderator reversal.* Another great listening aid is to ask a respondent to be the moderator for a question or two. Have one or two respondents ask questions of the group. Often respondents have a totally different frame of reference on a topic. Say to the group, "I've asked a lot of questions about what it means to have a clean house. If you became the moderator, write down one question you'd ask the group about a clean house that we haven't discussed." The moderator would then ask various respondents to pose their question to the group, and new or fresh thoughts that emerge would be probed.

These techniques not only force the moderator to listen better, but they generate an active and involved group. They also provide snippets of time for the moderator to think ahead and plan where to take the group next.

PROBING

Bar none, the most important skill that separates great moderators from the rest is knowing when and how to probe. They know or sense when it is important to dig below the answers that respondents give because there is more to be learned.

In every focus group, there are hundreds of opportunities to probe. After asking a general question and getting a response, probably the one probe that moderators use most with a respondent is "Why do you say that?" "Why do you say that?" is the beginning of what is referred to as a "question ladder." If you ask a respondent "Why do you say that?" multiple times (two, three, four times), you will find a wealth of information in their remarks. For example:

Respondent: I love driving my car fast.

Moderator: Why do you say that?

Respondent: Because it gives me a sense of freedom.

Moderator: Why do you say that?

Respondent: Well, I guess because there is no one around to tell me what to do.

Moderator: Why do you say that?

Respondent: Because my wife hates it when I drive fast. When she's not with me, I can pretend I'm Mario Andretti.

"Why do you say that?" probes help to get to deeper levels of attitudes and feelings and to surface thoughts and ideas that aren't easily or quickly expressed. In this case, the comment "I love driving my car fast" is so vague that it begs for probing and clarification. The final ladder probe surfaces a whole racecar frame of reference that would never have emerged otherwise.

Another example of probing is to use the answer that a respondent gives as the basis for another question. Here is an example of answer probing:

Moderator: Why do you brew coffee at home on some mornings but go to Starbucks for coffee on other mornings?

Respondent: I don't know. Just for a change of pace.

Moderator: What do you mean by change of pace?

Respondent: On some mornings I might have a little more time to sit and relax. Even though I brew Starbucks coffee at home, it never seems to be as good. So I go to the Starbucks up the block.

Moderator: Beside the coffee, is there anything else you like about sitting and relaxing at a Starbucks?

Respondent: When I leave Starbucks, I'm more ready for the day. I just feel a little more energized than when I have coffee at home.

You can see that the moderator probed every answer the respondent gave by turning it into another question. This probing surfaced the idea of being energized when having coffee at Starbucks, rather than at home, which could be an interesting advertising concept that Starbucks might wish to explore further.

When probing, it is also appropriate to question more than one respondent on a subject. Take the following:

John: I love shopping at Lands' End because the clothes fit me so well.

Moderator: Norman, what is it about the fit of clothes at Lands' End?

Norman: They fit in a way that makes me feel like I'm roaming Africa on a safari-kind of loose but relaxed.

Moderator: Harry, do you get that loose and relaxed feeling when you wear Lands' End clothes?

Harry: Not exactly loose and relaxed. I'd describe it as casual, you know, not pretentious.

Probing across respondents has the effect of keeping everyone involved in the conversation. In using this technique, care should be taken not to push respondents who find that the areas being probed have little to do with what may be important to them.

Here are a few guidelines to indicate when further probing is appropriate:

1. when you're getting the same answers over and over again – your questions are likely to be superficial;
2. when the answers you're getting fail to suggest actions that you feel you are likely to take;
3. when your gut tells you there's more to it than is being expressed;
4. when your experience indicates that what respondents are saying fails to result in added sales;
5. when you know that answers really exist in nuanced attitudes;
6. when you are looking for something that might produce a paradigm shift;
7. when you simply become bored with the answers you are getting.

Probing is very much an art and is best done by feel. The greater the experience moderators have in a product category, the more they are able to pick up areas that are ripe for probing. When respondents give unusual or out-of-the-ordinary responses, they will jump out at an experienced moderator and be cause for probing and digging deeper for the real meaning.

Being good at probing will come in time. You can speed up the process if you listen to the audiotapes of your groups. In doing so, you'll be amazed at the times you failed to seize on a respondent's remark and where probing could have added greatly to your learning.

KNOWING WHEN TO CHANGE SUBJECTS

Beating a topic to death should always be avoided. When questioning and probing on a subject ceases to be productive, it is both aggravating to respondents and a waste of valuable group time. Knowing when you have reached that point is the trick. You can sense that happening when:

1. you have given all the respondents a chance to respond to the same basic set of questions and feel that you can now summarize their collective feelings and opinions;
2. all the respondents give basically the same response when you ask a question;
3. you have tried to probe a topic by rephrasing and you don't get any new information;
4. you are able to anticipate what respondents will say before they say it;
5. you sense respondents getting fidgety and losing interest.

Knowing when to move from one topic to another comes from "feeling" the group. Respondents will let you know when they have more to say on a subject. They may shake their heads in agreement or disagreement when another respondent is talking or be inclined to interrupt because they are anxious to say something. They might pick up on the comments of each other and start talking before you have to ask a question.

When any of these things happen, you'll know that the group is engaged and has more to say. In fact, when this happens, the group is actually doing much of the work. The moderator then becomes the referee whose job it is to make sure everyone gets heard.

Another important point in moving off a topic is to know how much time you have. In developing a discussion guide, some topics will be far more important than others. Most moderators will anticipate the time they should spend with each topic and will move off a topic when the time allotment is reached. Below is the discussion guide that appeared earlier in this chapter (the note in bold shows how the moderator broke up the time allotted to each topic):

1. *Background* (**15 minutes total; complete by 15 minutes into the group**):
   - introductions, etc.;
   - likes/dislikes in purchasing wallpaper from catalogs;
   - whether recently purchased/considering purchase of wallpaper;
   - factors in determining whether to purchase from a catalog versus going to a retail store.

2. *Catalogs* (**25 minutes total; complete by 40 minutes into the group**):
    –   When wallpaper catalogs arrive in your home, what catches your attention? What makes you decide to look at some catalogs and not others?
    –   What is it about the cover that grabs your attention? What is it about some catalogs that causes you to look through them, while others are just glanced at?

    Probe importance:
    –   of a well-recognized name in the decision to inspect a wallpaper catalog when it arrives;
    –   of products being new, unique, and different from what might have been seen elsewhere;
    –   of price, clear descriptions;
    –   of companies that have their own credit plans in addition to normal credit cards;
    –   of being able to track the status of order by phone or online.

    Once you are satisfied with a catalog company, how important is price in the decision to purchase repeatedly from the same company. Would you continue to compare prices?

3. *Catalog companies* (**25 minutes total; complete by 65 minutes into the group**):
    –   Which wallpaper catalog companies are you aware of? Which companies have you purchased from? Why those?
    –   Which wallpaper catalog companies are you aware of but have not purchased from? Why those? What causes some to be purchased from but not others?
    –   List catalogs purchased from / aware of. Compare how they differ in terms of:
        –   quality of merchandise;
        –   ease of shopping;
        –   offering good prices / good promotions;
        –   customer service;
        –   reputation;
        –   price.

4. *Apex versus competition* (**55 minutes total; complete by the end of the group**):
    –   Pass out two Apex and two competitors' catalogs. Allow respondents 15 minutes to review. Have respondents make notes as to what they liked / disliked about each catalog.
    –   Rank the catalogs in terms of most to least compelling. Which catalog did you find most compelling? [Choose the most compelling.] Why that one? List the areas liked / disliked.

Probe:
- Does the catalog allow making a buying decision easy?
- In what ways is the catalog helpful?
- Is the catalog easy to read? In what ways?
- Is the catalog unique / different from the others? In what ways?
- How do you feel about the manner in which the products are shown and described? What about the quality of the photographs / product colors being true?
- What about the merchandised categories / depth and breadth of selection?
- What about the prices?
- If you wanted to place an order, could you do so without calling the number given for help? If not, what would you need to know?
- What additional information would you need to make a decision to purchase from the catalog?

Repeat the above process for the other three catalogs.

Within each of the above sections there are far more questions for you to ask than time would allow. Clearly, though, the purpose of the group is to probe deeply into the questions posed in Section 4. Belaboring other sections by asking superfluous or tangential questions once general attitudes have been covered would minimize time for Section 4 and would jeopardize the goal of the group.

The best way to know when to get off a topic is to know what you want to accomplish in the group. *Don't be tempted to spend time on a topic that is less than critical to the goals of the group. Don't be tempted to spend time on questions when you can predict how respondents will answer.*

FOLLOWING THE DISCUSSION GUIDE

The operative word here is "guide." Discussion guides are not questionnaires. When a questionnaire is administered to a respondent, it is done by the script, by rote. When a discussion guide is administered in a focus group, it is done creatively and with sensitivity to the goals of the group.

When you first look at a road map you're likely to get a general picture of the route to your destination. As your journey proceeds, you'll refer to the map again to make sure you haven't made a wrong turn. A discussion guide is like a road map, to be referred to occasionally and to make sure you are taking the group down the intended roads.

It is impossible to follow a discussion guide exactly as it is written. Conversations in focus groups don't go that way. So don't even try.

My experience with guides is that, while they are important, I don't refer to them much once a group begins. The guide will outline the areas to be covered and the general time allotted for exploring each area. It will also serve to embed in my memory the variety of questions I need to ask.

But the guide becomes almost superfluous after the first or second group of a four- or six-group study. That is, I tend to understand the patterns of thinking I'm likely to encounter if I don't vary my questions and approach. Therefore, I will put the guide aside and trust my questioning instincts.

Not all moderators like to work this way, and it certainly is not a great approach for a new moderator. There is comfort in following the guide more closely and not risking such freewheeling in a group. But it's essentially a matter of experience and style. There is no totally right or wrong approach. That's the message here.

When all is said and done, here's my take on using discussion guides:

- Look at Section 1 on introductions just before respondents enter the room. Note how much time you have and wait for everyone to be seated. Each introduction will take about 30 seconds, so plan accordingly.
- Look at the time you have for the next section of the guide. As the conversation unfolds, trust that the questions on the guide will be the ones that you'll ask naturally by just listening to the conversation. If your mind goes blank on what to ask next, look at the guide.
- Take a quick glance at the guide before you leave a section. If a compelling question pops up that you haven't covered, ask it. If not, move on.
- Keep track of the time. Note the topic of the next section, scan the first area of questioning on the guide, and dive in. If your mind goes blank, look at the guide.
- Don't be afraid to skip over a section. If you have completed Section 2 and it seems natural to skip Section 3 in favor of Section 4, jump ahead. Cover Section 3 at a later time.
- If you have certain group exercises or tasks to complete, look at the guide occasionally to remind yourself what you have in front of you (see the next section on group exercises).
- Give the guide one last glance a few minutes before the group is scheduled to end. Chances are you have covered almost everything that's important. If not, you still have time to go back.

Regard each group as a time to explore thoughts and ideas about general topics. Know that explorations can follow different paths and still reach the same destination. Discussion guides should be thought of as tools to aid in exploration, nothing more.

GROUP EXERCISES

Engaging respondents in exercises can be very productive. By exercises I am referring to periods of time in the group during which the moderator asks respondents to work on their own, in pairs, or in teams. Group exercises will change the pace of the session and are particularly useful when a group is dragging or nothing new seems to be emerging.

Group exercises can be either planned or spontaneous. If they are planned and part of the discussion guide, the moderator knows exactly when they should take place and how long they should last. If they are unplanned, the moderator will have to use on-the-spot judgment as to when an exercise should be tried and then instruct the group what to do.

Exercises can be productive when:

- looking for new ideas, needs, or wants;
- trying to determine the actions that you might take to change customer behavior;
- an advertisement, catalog, or other selling material is being critiqued;
- trying to develop a product or company personality;
- trying to determine product improvements.

Group exercises can also be used in a situation in which the moderator might be struggling or just be looking for a break to collect his or her thoughts on what the group seems to be saying.

Almost any exercise can be done individually, in pairs, or in teams:

- Individual exercises are valuable in forcing each respondent to think about the issues and becoming more active in group participation.
- Pair exercises are usually better in generating ideas and new approaches. Give-and-take situations are usually more productive for generating new ideas than having respondents work alone.
- Team exercises usually generate fewer ideas, thoughts, or approaches, but the ones that do emerge are usually better thought out or conceptualized.

There is no right and wrong approach here. Sometimes exercises surface the unexpected; sometimes they are totally unproductive.

Below are typical group exercises that can be done individually, in pairs, or in teams. Usually 5 to 10 minutes is appropriate for each exercise:

- *Write an ad for a product or company.* Have individuals or teams present the ad to the group and explain why they took the direction they did.

- *Create personality profiles.* Have a pile of totally disparate magazine pictures and put them in the middle of the conference table. Instruct individuals or teams to choose three to five pictures that they feel represent the personality of the company or product under study. Have respondents explain why they feel that the pictures they chose represent the personality of the company.
- *Look into the future.* Have individuals or teams write down what a company and product could do in five years that would make them want to buy. Have the ideas presented.
- *Create a wish list.* Have individuals or teams create and present wishes for the future as to how the company or product could make their life easier.
- *Critiquing.* Anything can be critiqued – an ad, catalog, product, or idea. Critiquing seems to take on greater depth when pairs or teams "conspire together." Have pairs or teams create a critique list and present their critiques and suggestions for improvements.

Group exercises are often less about the actual ideas (although sometimes a great idea will pop up) than they are about looking at the issues from various perspectives. Exercises often are best in stimulating moderator thinking and for suggesting new ideas or theories that should be explored further in the same group or with future groups.

PRE-GROUP HOMEWORK

Sometimes it is productive to have respondents think about a topic before they attend the group. Even though respondents will be screened to represent your target market, it is unrealistic to expect them to be familiar with all the issues that you are going to question them about.

Very often it is important to get spontaneous reactions and opinions from respondents. But other times it is far more productive to have respondents familiarize themselves with the topic before they come into the group. For example:

- You want to know how respondents feel about customer service in retail stores when they are shopping for diamonds, expensive electronic equipment, health foods – or anything else, for that matter. It can be extremely productive to have respondents visit several stores before they attend the group. In that way, the customer service experience will be current and fresh in their minds. They will be less speculative when making comments.

- You might be interested in how competitors package their products. If you're selling cosmetics, have respondents visit the cosmetic section of a store and purchase two packages they like and two they don't like (you would have to repay them for their purchases). When they bring their packages to the group, their task will be to compare and contrast the packages.
- Have respondents keep a diary. Perhaps you are trying to generate unmet needs in the kitchen. Instruct respondents to keep a seven-day diary writing down all the frustrating happenings as they go about preparing meals. It's often the little things that happen, and that are easily forgotten, that lead to breakthroughs. Having respondents keep a pre-group diary can be very productive.
- Have respondents bring in articles. Inform them of the topics that will be discussed in the group. Instruct them to watch the newspapers, browse magazines, or surf Google, and collect two articles that they find interesting about your topic. Use this material to stimulate conversation.

There are many circumstances that, by forcing respondents into your issues before they attend the group, can prove extremely productive. Remember, they aren't thinking about your problems the way you are. By encouraging them to do so, your learning curve will peak.

BUILDING FROM ONE GROUP TO ANOTHER

A focus group study is a series of dynamic building blocks. Each group will unveil new information and new ways to think about the issues. As moderators proceed from one group to the next, they're sensitive to the ever-changing and often – inconsistent attitudes that they hear.

What is always interesting is to explore from group to group the new theories that emerge and the challenge of figuring out why respondents with seemingly similar profiles have different attitudes and perspectives. Further, it is constructive to take concepts and ideas that one group thinks are good and explore them in subsequent groups. Always keep in mind that to conduct each group exactly the same way is missing the point.

A focus group study is about learning as you go. If that means deviating from the discussion guide, changing your approach to reflect what you are learning, or trying different group exercises, you should not hesitate to do so.

RECALL RESPONDENTS

Recalling respondents simply means having the same respondents return for a second or third session – or perhaps even more. This is not a popular focus group technique but that does not negate its potential effectiveness.

When you bring respondents in for a first group and question them, they'll express what spontaneously occurs to them in those two hours. For most focus group studies, this is enough. But when it comes to digging at unmet needs, wants, wishes, and desires, you won't be likely to get much that is new in those first couple of hours.

For the vast majority of purchases that consumers make, and particularly for less costly products, they aren't particularly concerned about your company, your products, or your services. Occasionally, they may read your selling material or the labels on your products. Most of the time, their purchases are by rote. They certainly don't think much about improvements you could make and, when asked in two-hour focus groups, they rarely think beyond the obvious.

When you clue in respondents and tell them what you are trying to accomplish, you peak their interest. You surface their awareness of your issues. You make them more sensitive to what you could do for them if you wish to improve your company, products, or services and make them more loyal to you.

Think of it this way. If I were to give you two hours to come up with a great new product that addresses a need that you don't even know you have, do you think you'd come up with much? Probably not! But if I gave you four, six, or eight hours and told you to take your time and be more aware and observant of your needs, do you think your chances for discovering new possibilities will improve? I do.

At many levels, two-hour focus groups are only a superficial probing of consumer attitudes and behavior. Try giving one or two groups diaries to complete or homework assignments after their first group, and then recall them in a week or two for a second session. At the recall session discuss their diaries, homework, and your issues. You'll be amazed at the new information that surfaces. You'll get ideas and suggestions that those same consumers didn't express in the first group simply because the ideas didn't occur to them the moment you asked.

Consumers are experts. Every time they make a purchase they express their expertise. Recall groups help you get closer to understanding what makes them tick and how to change their attitudes and behavior. To not take advantage of that expertise is a qualitative research waste.

USING THE RESULTS OF FOCUS GROUPS

Just for emphasis, let me say again that you should not place reliance solely on the results from focus group studies as a basis for action. They provide grounding for a better understanding of the issues. They allow you to frame the scope of the problem.

Yet I have known many companies that use the results of focus groups to make wholesale changes or drastically alter their strategies. These include shifts in the way they advertise, product formulation changes, or allocating huge sums of money for the introduction of a new product. Sometimes these decisions work out successfully and sometimes they are a total disaster. If you can afford to be wrong by jumping to conclusions from focus groups, go right ahead. Maybe you'll just get lucky.

But that is just it. You'll be relying on luck.

The only time I'd suggest that you should use the results from focus groups to make major decisions is if you're going to make a decision without any research at all. I will be the first to admit that, as many times as focus groups have failed to point the right direction, I have seen them say exactly the same thing as has been discovered through a costly follow-up survey.

In fact, it's always been interesting to me that, when a client has conducted a number of focus group studies and follow-up surveys, both my client and I develop a better sense for using focus group findings. Making decisions based on focus groups alone seems to be less risky. And knowing when not to jump is also more obvious. Until that happens for you, tread lightly on your focus group findings.

The more experience you have with focus groups, the better you'll become in interpreting the results. You'll develop a feel. You'll know when risking action is indicated over being cautious and conducting a follow-up survey. You'll understand how the results from focus groups will sharpen your decision making and help you make wiser choices.

When all is said and done, though, market conditions and the need to act can be very real – when waiting is not an option or when doing nothing is far worse than doing a few focus groups. There are times when conducting a focus group study is your only option before you must act. To this I'd say, do the groups. Focus groups by themselves will indeed reduce your risks.

TYPES OF QUALITATIVE RESEARCH

When considering the types of qualitative research that are best for your situation, there aren't a great number of options to confuse you. By far the most popular is the traditional focus group. Listed below are the various qualitative methodologies and the advantages and disadvantages of each.

Traditional focus groups

Characteristics:

- usually scheduled for two hours in length;
- consist of 8 to 10 respondents;
- tend to focus on a homogeneous customer or prospect targets for each group;
- consist of four groups for the typical study although six, eight, or even more can be beneficial.

Advantages:

- allow give-and-take interaction-dynamic;
- allow a wide number of topics to be discussed and probed;
- provide a learn-as-you-go atmosphere – new ideas and theories evolve and are quickly explored, improved, or discarded;
- great for providing background or "first blush" information on topics of interest;
- fun, and allow easy observation by others in the company and fodder for decision making;
- can be completed quickly, usually in less than a month;
- generally less expensive than survey research techniques.

Disadvantages:

- tendency to jump to conclusions;
- not projectable – limited decision making is always prudent;
- can be biased toward "groupthink" in that some respondents are swayed by the opinions of others;
- can be dominated by respondents who are overly opinionated or verbal.

Mini focus groups

Characteristics: the same as focus groups, except that each mini group consists of 4 to 6 respondents instead of 8 to 10.

Advantages:

- the same as focus groups, but lower number of respondents per group, making them less expensive;
- lower cost per group, and therefore more economical to add additional target segments that might otherwise be unaffordable.

Disadvantages:

- lower number of respondents per group can render the session *somewhat* less dynamic;
- information provided could be less robust.

Recall focus groups

Characteristics:

- the same characteristics as traditional or mini groups;
- respondents recruited to attend two or more groups;
- homework assigned between groups;
- incentives not paid to the respondents until the completion of the final group.

Advantages:

- respondents become more aware of why they behave as they do;
- more effective at surfacing unmet needs, wishes, wants, and desires that are not immediately evident;
- greater rapport developed with respondents so that they become comfortable expressing themselves and their ideas;
- more effective than traditional focus groups when developing new ideas, products, or services.

Disadvantages:

- expectation should be tempered – sometimes recall groups don't produce anything new or worthwhile;
- take longer to complete than traditional focus group studies.

One-on-one interviews

Characteristics:

- one respondent at a time is interviewed;
- usually scheduled for one hour or less in length;
- typical study can consist of anywhere from 12 to 48 or more interviews.

Advantages:

- sensitive and personal topics more easily explored;
- lack of group pressure provides an atmosphere in which respondents can express their thoughts honestly and independently;
- allow greater in-depth probing of each respondent.

Disadvantages:

- lack of dynamic interchange – ideas and theories expressed are not as easily explored or challenged;
- time-consuming.

Dyads or triads

Characteristics:

- respondents interviewed two or three at a time;
- usually scheduled for one hour or less in length;
- typical studies can consist of anywhere from 12 to 24 dyads or triads.

Advantages:

- can be more dynamic than one-on-one interviews, as thoughts and ideas of one respondent can be commented upon by another;
- lack of traditional group pressure – provide a more easy-going atmosphere in which respondents can express their thoughts honestly and independently;
- allow greater in-depth probing of each respondent;
- more economical to explore the attitudes of a wider number of targets.

Disadvantages:

- lack the full dynamics of traditional focus groups – ideas and theories expressed are not as easily explored or challenged;
- time-consuming.

CREATIVE CONSUMERS

A great deal of research has been conducted on the subject of creativity. Edward de Bono's book entitled *Serious Creativity* (Harper Business, 1992) is a wonderful read. You can also go to www.synectics.com to find out everything you might want to know from one of the earliest pioneers on the subject of creativity.

Suffice it to say, almost anyone can be trained to be more creative. Given the right circumstances and training, most people can generate more new ideas than they ever thought possible.

Nevertheless, some people are more naturally gifted in creative thinking – quicker on the creative trigger. Finding such creative thinkers among focus group respondents is not that difficult. About 15 to 20 percent of respondents who qualify for your focus groups will also qualify as being creative consumers.

If you are conducting qualitative research to develop new products, services, or ideas, or are just seeking a deeper level of understanding regarding unmet consumer needs, you should consider recruiting one or more groups with creative respondents.

To do so, first screen your respondents to make sure that they are in your target. Then, using the questionnaire shown in Table 9.1, ask respondents the extent to which they agree or disagree with each statement.

What you will find with creative consumers is that they are more verbal, expressive, and able to speculate about issues. They are more aggressive and opinionated than normal respondents. As such, keeping a group of creative consumers under control can be a challenge for new moderators.

Nevertheless, the ideas that emerge from creative consumers often provide extraordinary fodder, especially when you are trying to stretch beyond the obvious. This can be extremely useful when your study calls for exploring emerging trends or trying to determine the needs, wants, wishes, and desires that will start a new trend.

There are other qualitative approaches, such as focus group panels and observational and in-home videotaping studies, but these tend to be useful to the more seasoned user of qualitative research. It is prudent get a good

Table 9.1 Recruiting creative respondents

	Agree strongly	Agree somewhat	Disagree somewhat	Disagree strongly
1. You are a very energetic person	4	3	2	1
2. People say you have a great sense of humor	4	3	2	1
3. You are comfortable discussing concepts or ideas you may not be familiar with	4	3	2	1
4. You are open to new ideas and activities more than other people	4	3	2	1
5. Others describe you as persistent	4	3	2	1
6. You often dream or fantasize	4	3	2	1
7. You enjoy the uncertainty that often comes with working through a problem	4	3	2	1
8. You always like to be the first in your area to try something new	4	3	2	1
9. You would describe your childhood as unpredictable	4	3	2	1
10. You often think of solutions to problems when you least expect them	4	3	2	1
11. You often say things spontaneously without thinking	4	3	2	1
12. You enjoy making up stories	4	3	2	1

Total respondent score ____ Maximum score = 48 (12 statements × 4)

A respondent must score 36 or more to qualify as being a creative thinker.

grounding in the basic approaches previously outlined before moving to these more sophisticated methods.

In summary, qualitative research is an extremely valuable research tool, especially for those new to research. It can surface the many issues that might be addressed to grow a business and it can do so inexpensively. Importantly, it can focus attention on both the short- and long-term issues that need attention and, in doing so, can provide impetus for growth. But it is an easy tool to abuse.

In developing a research program for your company, use qualitative research prudently and sparingly. Understand its value and its limitations. Don't be lulled into thinking that, because you have conducted focus groups or other qualitative research, you have done your homework.

What you have done is to begin the research process. For that, I offer my congratulations. But at the same time, I hope you won't end your search at this point.

10

Brainstorming and other ideation processes

At some point, you have probably had experience with brainstorming – the groupthink technique where anything goes, no ideas are barred, and nothing is too silly or stupid to express.

I have mixed feelings about brainstorming. On the one hand, brainstorming sessions are popular, easy to convene, and usually generate a lot of ideas. On the other hand, the ideas generated tend to be superficial and not particularly unique.

There are several reasons that brainstorming sessions are often unproductive. Usually the length of time that they last, two to four hours, is inadequate. Just as ideas are taking shape, the session is over. Further, it takes a certain level of training and practice to understand fully the rules for an effective brainstorming session. The typical brainstorming group just doesn't invest much energy in learning the rules of creativity in order to optimize the session.

Nevertheless, many Guerrillas new to research might also be new to brainstorming. Just as conducting research for the first time will open your eyes, the act of convening a brainstorming team in your company or among your customers can do the same. If it does no more than serve as a forum for revisiting old ideas that still have merit, it will be time well spent, and you just might surface new ideas that your employees and customers haven't suggested because they haven't had the forum for doing so.

Here are some simple rules to follow when conducting a brainstorming session:

- *Appoint a recorder.* This is a person who stands at an easel and writes down the ideas that are expressed. The recorder usually refrains from writing down his or her own ideas. The recorder should be impartial to the ideas expressed while making sure that participants follow the rules of the session. For company brainstorming sessions, it is often best for the recorder to be the boss or the highest-ranking person in the room. This sends the message that the boss is not trying to sway the group one way or the other and is truly interested in ideas other than his or her own.

- *Agreement.* Only people who want to be in a brainstorming session should attend. Shrinking violets or those with an ax to grind will inhibit the group. There must be tacit agreement that hidden agendas will be shelved and that judgment will be put aside.

- *Safe space.* A brainstorming session will be unproductive if participants feel that the ideas they express might be used against them or in any way reflect on them negatively. The highest-ranking person should assure everyone on this essential issue.

- *Suspend judgment and suspend "Yes, buts."* In business, people "Yes, but" each other to death. In the normal course of business, someone will come up with a thought or idea, and it is quite normal for others immediately to judge it. An idea will be expressed and someone will say, "Yes, but we tried that last year" or "Yes, but that will cost too much." "Yes, buts" will kill a brainstorming session. Therefore, it is essential for the recorder to listen carefully for "Yes, buts" and to remind participants not to judge ideas. Idea-bashing is the fastest way to an ineffective brainstorming session.

- *"What do I like about it?"* Ideas will prosper and grow once a group moves from "Yes, but" thinking to "What do I like about it?" thinking. The sooner the group learns to express what they like about ideas, the better the ideas will become. When an idea is expressed, the recorder should ask the group to express their positives about the idea and how it can be made better.

- *Listen and write.* The best ideas often surface when others are talking. Active listening is the act of paying rapt attention to ideas expressed by others and writing down ideas that come to your mind when others are talking. The recorder should continually encourage participants to listen to what is being said and to write down their ideas that pop to mind.

- *Have fun.* The very nature of new ideas is that they often sound funny, silly, or stupid when they are first expressed. Usually, ideas that are silly are the very ones that are new and that should be nurtured. Learn to judge the effectiveness of a brainstorming session by the amount of fun and laughter that is present. More fun invariably equates to better ideas.

The above rules are basic to an effective brainstorming session. But there are many approaches to brainstorming and many websites available on brainstorming. Check http://www.jpb.com/creative/brainstorming.php for one such site, or go to any search engine and type in "brainstorming."

In addition to brainstorming, there are also other techniques for generating new ideas and a variety of companies that specialize in ideation processes. Again, check any of the search engines using the key words "new product idea generation" and you will find a multitude of companies that you might consider. Some of the processes that you will find include:

- more intensely focused brainstorming processes that last one or more days;
- processes that include workshops and interactive sessions with customers or prospects;
- processes that include developing graphic depictions or actual development of new products or prototypes;
- processes that include secondary source searches, homework assignments, and use of other stimulus material to generate ideas;
- processes that include training in creativity and how to look beyond the obvious when generating ideas;
- over-time processes that last for months, thus expanding the time frame for generating ideas.

But this isn't a book about brainstorming or idea generation, so I won't belabor this subject. I will leave the brainstorming topic with this:

- Brainstorming or other ideation processes can be an effective tool for generating ideas and, thus, can motivate fresh thinking. Whether such thinking proves to be productive is something else.
- Ideas coming out of brainstorming or other ideation processes almost always need a reality check. Whether they, in fact, address consumer needs or wants that aren't already being addressed is generally the issue.
- Most ideas from brainstorming or other ideation processes need to be reworked from a consumer perspective. Focus groups can provide such a perspective.
- Creativity isn't summoned on demand. Therefore, ideation processes that expand the typical brainstorming time frame are more likely to produce ideas that have greater potential.

- Ideation should be ongoing. When participants are regularly involved in generating new ideas, they are more attuned to the world and to unmet needs, wishes, wants, and desires that exist. They become aware of the little things that can make all the difference in discovering a breakthrough idea. Having a continual forum for expressing and building on ideas is extremely important.
- Rarely, if ever, is it wise to commit sizeable sums of money to developing ideas that come from brainstorming or ideation processes without first conducting a quantitative survey to determine the degree of consumer interest in the ideas that you are considering.

No matter what technique you use to develop new ideas, concepts, or products, attitude research should be integral to the process. Ninety percent of the time it will be a terrible waste of time and money to plough ahead with great-sounding ideas that come from brainstorming until research is used to assess the potential for those ideas.

11

Surveys

The term "quantitative research" is synonymous with *survey* research. Quantitative research – surveys – puts numbers behind the issues. Unlike qualitative research – focus groups and the like – quantitative research will tell you how many people think one way or the other.

A focus group study will highlight potential issues, such as customer service, price, or product variety, as being the ones that could be addressed to increase sales. A survey will tell you which one of the issues is the most important to increasing sales, which is second most important, which is third most important, and so forth.

Ultimately, it does you little good simply to know that there is potential for more profits if you were to take action to improve customer service, change your product, or lower you price. Without knowing which one would have the greatest impact, you would have to take action to improve all of them at the same time. Why, for example, would you cut prices without knowing that it would motivate only 10 percent of your customers to buy more, whereas improving customer service would motivate 50 percent? You wouldn't – or you shouldn't.

Survey research is projectable research. That means that the results can be generalized to the population as a whole. From a survey that might question as few as 150 respondents, you can confidently predict what is important for many thousands. That means that you can determine which actions will be most potent in motivating which targets – and to what extent.

Surveys allow you to set priorities based on the number of customers or prospects in your target market who would be most influenced by your action.

TYPES OF SURVEYS

As previously discussed, there are two general areas of survey research: strategic and tactical.

Strategic studies provide a global understanding of the marketplace. They generate essential learning regarding attitudes, images, and perceptions that consumers have toward the companies, brands, and products that compete against each other. They determine the extent to which the needs, wants, wishes, and desires of customers and prospects are being met, and which companies are doing the best job of meeting them.

The information generated from strategic studies forms the basis for determining the marketing direction a company should take – the position that, if achieved, offers the greatest opportunity for success.

Tactical studies address specific questions and issues. Once the overall marketing strategy and desired position are determined, there are many smaller elements that contribute to ultimate success. Tactical studies determine which elements are strongest in achieving the strategy or where changes should be made to reinforce the strategy.

Consider the many tactical studies that you might conduct:

- *customer satisfaction* studies, which determine how customers and prospects are being served and what should be done to serve them better;
- *tracking* studies, which determine whether you are achieving your desired image, position, and strategy, and how your competition might be hindering your success;
- *product development* studies, which determine the new products or services that reinforce your strategic direction;
- *product improvement* studies, which determine what can be done to improve current products and services to keep them up to date and competitive;
- *pricing* studies, which determine how much you can charge for your products or services;
- *advertising awareness* studies, which determine whether your advertising messages are being seen, heard, and remembered, and whether the advertising is motivating customers to purchase more frequently and/or changing the attitudes of prospects so that they'll soon begin purchasing;
- *advertising communication* studies, which determine the strongest messages for communicating your company, brand, or product strategy and for motivating purchase;
- *premium or promotion* studies, which determine the best kinds of special offers that will motivate purchase and reinforce your *strategic* goals;

- *packaging* studies, which determine the strongest package and graphic approach that is on strategy to motivate purchase of your products;
- *naming* studies, which determine the strongest name for your company, product, brand, or service and is in keeping with your strategic direction;
- *screening* studies, which determine which among a number of potential new products or services offers the best option for expanding your marketplace and reinforcing your strategy.

While tactical studies are important, strategic studies are the essential building block to understanding the marketplace and how to compete effectively. Think about it as if you were taking an exam without first doing your homework. Maybe you'll pass, but the odds of achieving a high grade are greatly diminished. Without a well-structured strategic research study, without doing basic homework, your decisions are often based on best guess or, even worse, on conjecture and hope.

Tactical studies are most effective if they are conducted within the global context provided by a strategic study. To determine the best package that communicates quality, for example, is moot if strategy dictates that the most effective package should be one that communicates low price.

If you don't know where you're going, no road will get you there.

STRATEGIC STUDY OBJECTIVES

You have decided that you want to conduct a strategic study to understand your marketplace "drivers." You want to determine the factors that are important in keeping your customers or attracting your competitors' customers. Such background studies are often referred to as "segmentation studies," "usage and attitude studies," or "awareness and attitude studies" – or simply call it your "homework study."

To get started with your homework study, develop a short statement of the strategic objective. This will help you focus your study emphasis. Follow the example below, which is written as the strategic objective for a window air-conditioner study: "To determine the attributes that are important when consumers purchase window air-conditioners. An additional objective is to determine how my company and my competitors perform relative to the important attributes."

Stating the strategic objective in this way focuses the study in two areas: 1) determining the important air-conditioner attributes to customers in general; and 2) determining company performance on the attributes.

Another strategic objective statement might be: "To determine the segments of consumers that exist in the air-conditioner marketplace, and which attributes are important in appealing to each segment. An additional objective is to determine whether some companies do a better job of appealing to a certain segment of customers than to others (e.g., those who lives in big homes as opposed to small apartments, etc.)."

Stating the strategic objective in this manner broadens the scope of the study in that it must now: 1) seek to determine the various *segments* of the market that exist and array the attributes by two or more customer segments; and 2) determine whether some companies perform better when appealing to the various segments than others.

Whatever the strategic objective, it should point out the preeminent goal of the study. Only when you are clear on the strategic objective can you elaborate by stating the secondary objectives of the study.

The following are good examples of secondary objectives for a strategic study of the window air-conditioner market:

- What specific attributes are most important and least important when it comes to the purchase of window air-conditioners?
- Which brands are purchased?
- How is each brand rated in regard to how it is perceived to deliver the various attributes?
- What attributes are not being strongly addressed in the marketplace and would therefore provide an opportunity to gain a competitive advantage?
- What brands are perceived as doing the weakest job in delivering important attributes to their customers and, therefore, would be the most vulnerable to a competitor?

Developing clear and concise objectives is not an academic exercise. It is essential in determining your final study methodology and its likely cost. If you are crystal clear on the information that you seek, you will not over-spend to collect superfluous data or underspend and find out later that the research only took you half way.

DETERMINING YOUR TARGET RESPONDENTS

A critical step in designing a survey research project is the determination of whose opinions are important – that is, determining the profile of your desired targets. Do you want to gather data on men versus women or younger versus older respondents? Perhaps the attitudes of respondents who have purchased from your company once as opposed to those purchasing many times are important. Or maybe you want respondents who are heavy buyers of your products compared to light buyers.

There could be dozens of target respondents whom it is important to study. Without careful determination of your targets, you could end up with a wealth of data among respondents that offer little potential for growth.

12

Writing questionnaires

When writing questionnaires, it is worth keeping Gerry Linda's advice in mind:

> Never ask a question because it might be good to know or because you've seen other questionnaires with the same question. Only ask those questions for which you know what decision you will make when the data comes in and where the findings will influence marketing decision making or consumer behavior. Asking any other questions only wastes money and time – your money and the time of the respondents.

A survey cannot be completed without a questionnaire. Unlike a focus group discussion guide that is used as a dynamic tool for questioning respondents, a survey questionnaire is precisely structured and must be followed exactly. When an interviewer administers a questionnaire it is done precisely as it is written. There is no deviation from the questionnaire or room for interpretation. Questions are asked exactly as they are written.

There are two major considerations when writing a questionnaire: 1) whether the questionnaire will be administered by an interviewer directly to the respondent; and 2) whether the questionnaire will be completed by the respondent without assistance from an interviewer – a self-administered questionnaire.

An interviewer-administered questionnaire can be quite complex. Because interviewers are trained in the flow of the questionnaires they administer and will conduct a number of practice interviews prior to confronting a respondent, developing a complex questionnaire that is interviewer administered is not a problem.

Often interviewer-administered questionnaires will have skip patterns that jump a respondent from one section of the questionnaire to another based on their responses. Sometimes, particularly with face-to-face interviews, the questioning process might also involve showing respondents certain products or exhibits during the interview or having the respondents read concepts or ideas based on how they respond to various questions.

Self-administered questionnaires should be simple, straightforward, and logical. Question 2 should follow question 1. Question 3 should follow question 2, and so forth. The going-in assumption with self-administered questionnaires should be that respondents will not complete a questionnaire when the pages are crowded or hard to read, or when instructions for completion are overly complex.

It has been estimated that as many as 50 percent of respondents who start a self-administered questionnaire will not complete it because they become irritated and annoyed at the way it is constructed. When writing a self-administered questionnaire, then, every care must be taken to ensure that it is easy to complete and that it answers itself.

Self-administered questionnaires should be written with a child's mentality in mind.

A word of advice

It is not easy to write an effective questionnaire. It takes practice and experience. But that doesn't mean you shouldn't try. With careful reading of this chapter, you will have the tools to write a workable questionnaire.

But you should always consider hiring a research professional to review your questionnaires to check for clarity and flow and to ensure that you are asking the kinds of questions that address your study objectives. It shouldn't take a professional more than a couple of hours of time and will be money very well spent.

TYPES OF QUESTIONS

Survey questionnaires are primarily *closed-end* in nature. That is, the answers are pre-structured. Closed-end questions are those for which the interviewer reads the question and the response options are predetermined. Here is an example of a closed-end question with the optional answers:

How would you rate Exxon as a company? Do you feel it is:
- a superior company
- an excellent company
- a good company
- a fair company
- a poor company

As is evident, there are only five possible responses to the above question.

Other survey questions could be *open-ended* in nature. With open-ended questions there are no structured answers. The interviewer records the respondent's verbatim comments to the question. An example would be:

How do you feel about Exxon as a company?

Both questioning techniques allow answers to be tabulated and the exact number of respondents giving particular answers can be reported.

As you read the remainder of this chapter, keep in mind that there are only two types of survey questions, closed-end and open-ended.

QUESTIONNAIRES FOR TELEPHONE AND PERSONAL INTERVIEWING

The flow of a questionnaire to be used for telephone or personal interviewing always begins with an introduction followed by a series of *screening questions*. The introduction is to gain respondent cooperation in the interview. The screening questions are to determine whether the respondent is qualified to be interviewed.

Telephone and personal interview questionnaires have a distinct flow – or distinct phases. They are:

1. the *cooperation* phase;
2. the respondent *qualification* phase;
3. the *main body* of the questionnaire phase;
4. the *demographic* phase;
5. the *thank-you* phase.

THE COOPERATION PHASE

Step 1 involves gaining respondent cooperation to be interviewed. Because respondents are usually skeptical when first approached, what you say and how you say it can make the difference between a quick "No, thanks" and the opportunity to complete an interview.

First off, with telephone interviews, the person who answers the phone may clearly not be the person you want to interview (e.g., a man answers and you want to interview a woman, or perhaps a child answers). The best approach is simply to ask to speak to the male or female head of household. If the person answering asks who is calling, simply say that it is about doing a market research interview.

Once you have a male or female who might qualify for the interview, you can use several approaches to gain respondent cooperation:

Introduction #1. Hello, my name is _____ from [insert the name of the research company conducting the interview], a national market research firm. I want to assure you that this is not a sales call of any kind, and no one will try to sell you anything as a result of your cooperation. May I have a few minutes of your time? Thank you.

Comment: The goal here is to quickly assure the person that you aren't selling anything. While this is a standard approach and is usually effective, should you feel that different wording would be better to accomplish this goal you should use it.

Introduction #2. Hello, my name is _____ from [insert the name of the research company conducting the interview]. We are conducting a market research study on the topic of [insert the topic] that will last about [insert the time frame]. I want to assure you that this is not a sales call of any kind, and no one will try to sell you anything as a result of your cooperation. May I have a few minutes of your time? Thank you.

Comment: Most researchers prefer to be up front with a potential respondent about the topic and length of interview. While some respondents will terminate an interview when they learn of the topic or when they learn how long the interview will take, it is better that a respondent doesn't start the interview than hang up when it is half-completed because it's taking too long. I generally prefer to use introduction #2.

Introduction #3. Hello, my name is _____ from [insert the name of the research company conducting the interview]. We are conducting a market research study for [insert the sponsor of the research]. The topic of the study is [insert the topic], and the interview will last about [insert the time frame].

Comment: Informing the respondent of the sponsor of the study will usually enhance cooperation. As will be discussed later in this chapter, though, in many cases it is desirable to keep the name of the sponsor confidential. Where confidentiality is not an issue or it is perhaps even desirable to disclose the sponsor's identity, use introduction #3.

THE QUALIFICATION PHASE

Once you have respondent agreement for an interview, there will be a series of questions to determine whether, in fact, you have a qualified respondent. This is referred to as the "screening phase." Just as in focus groups, most survey questionnaires have a critical industry screening question. This immediately eliminates people whose attitudes might be biased or who are in a competitive industry and might use the fact that you are conducting a survey to their advantage. For example, if you were conducting a study among customers who shop for computers, you would use the following critical industry screening questions:

Are you, or is any member of your household, employed in the computer industry, such as a manufacturer, distributor, or retailer of computers? IF YES, TERMINATE.

Are you or is any member of your family employed in marketing, advertising, or the marketing research industry? IF YES, TERMINATE.

Comment: In this case, the study is about computers and the types of people indicated above would be deemed inappropriate for interview. You would, of course, have to determine whether either of these screening questions is necessary for your study and insert the appropriate wording.

Once you have eliminated critical industry respondents, you may still have other screening questions to make sure that the person is qualified to complete the questionnaire. Below is a screening question that might be used if you were conducting a study for a bank about checking accounts:

Are you the person in your household who is most responsible for determining the bank you use for your checking account? IF NOT, ASK TO SPEAK TO THAT PERSON.

Comment: If necessary for your study, now is the time to ask whatever questions are appropriate to make sure you are talking to the right person. Whether it's a consumer, professional, or business-to-business interview, you don't want to waste time questioning a respondent further only to find that the person isn't the decision maker.

At this point, you have generated respondent cooperation and determined that the person doesn't pose a critical industry problem and is indeed the decision maker. So far, so good!

But there still may be a number of additional screening questions that should be asked before you reach the main body of the interview. These questions are determined by your target market requirements and your determination of who it is important to interview. There can be any number of screening questions that are necessary to qualify a target respondent. The following are some examples:

Additional screening question #1. In the past 90 days, have you personally purchased office products or supplies for your household? IF NO, TERMINATE.

Comment: If you are representing an office products company, you might want to interview only respondents who have purchased office products and supplies in the past 90 days. Therefore, screening question #1 would be asked, which qualifies the respondent as appropriate to interview.

Additional screening question #2. Are you between the ages of 25 and 45? IF NO, TERMINATE.

Comment: If you want to interview only respondents in a certain age range you would use an age-screening question such as question #2.

Additional screening question #3. What one brand of gasoline do you use most often? IF THE SPONSOR YOU ARE REPRESENTING (e.g., SHELL) IS NOT MENTIONED, TERMINATE.

Comment: Often the study will call for the interviewing of respondents who use a certain brand or product. In such a case, a brand-screening question would be asked, like additional screening question #3.

Additional screening question #4. In the next three months, are you very likely or not very likely to shop for a new computer? IF NOT VERY LIKELY, TERMINATE.

Comment: If you want to interview respondents who are likely to take some kind of purchase action in the near future, a screening question is required. In question #4, the goal is to interview only respondents who are very likely to shop for a new computer in the next three months. You would, of course, choose the screening time frame most appropriate for you.

> *Additional screening question #5.* In the past six months, have you spent at least $200 purchasing wine for use in your home or to give as a gift? IF NO, TERMINATE.

Comment: You might want to qualify respondents who have committed a significant amount of money to purchasing products in your product category. Additional screening question #5 indicates that the target respondent must have spent at least $200 on wine in the past six months.

Again, to identify a target respondent, there are often several screening questions that are required. You might want your respondents to be in a certain age group as well as to be heavy purchasers. You could qualify respondents as having a certain favorite brand but also likely to try a new brand in the next three months.

In determining your target respondents, you should use as many screening questions as are necessary to identify only those people whose opinions you seek.

Setting quotas with screening questions

Many market research studies are designed to develop information for two or more targets – that is, for two or more groups that have different screening qualifications. In such cases, quotas are determined. Quotas refer to the number of interviews that you want to collect among various target segments.

Screening questions will also allow you to determine the appropriate quota group for a respondent.

For example, look at additional screening question #3 again:

> What one brand of gasoline do you use most often? IF SHELL IS NOT MENTIONED, TERMINATE.

Your study might call for conducting 150 interviews among people indicating Shell is the brand that they use most often and 150 interviews among people indicating they purchase another brand most often. While your screening question would be the same as originally written, instead of terminating the respondent you would have a different instruction, as follows:

What one brand of gasoline do you use most often? QUOTA: COMPLETE 150 INTERVIEWS AMONG SHELL MOST OFTEN AND 150 AMONG OTHER BRANDS MOST OFTEN.

Take another example in which the goal is to screen a variety of targets:

When you use copying and printing services outside your home, do you usually use:
– Alpha-Graphics or other printing chains like Kwik Kopy, PIP, Sir Speedy, etc.
– Kinko's
– OfficeMax
– Office Depot
– Staples
– A local print shop
QUOTA GROUP #1: CONDUCT 150 INTERVIEWS AMONG THOSE WHO USUALLY USE KINKO'S. QUOTA GROUP #2: CONDUCT 150 INTERVIEWS AMONG THOSE WHO USUALLY USE A LOCAL PRINT SHOP. QUOTA GROUP #3: CONDUCT 150 INTERVIEWS AMONG THOSE WHO USUALLY USE ALL OTHERS.

In both of the above examples, every person initially screened will qualify to be interviewed and will fall into a quota group. Respondents will only be terminated when 150 interviews in a quota group are collected and a respondent is identified who is no longer needed to fill a quota.

As you can see, the screening phase of the questionnaire can be an involved process. It can require any number of questions and often takes several minutes to complete. But careful thought to the screening process is essential for a successful survey.

Once you have written your screening questions, always go back and check them against your target respondent requirements. If they do not precisely identify the types of respondents you wish to interview, add or reword questions until they do.

THE MAIN BODY OF THE QUESTIONNAIRE PHASE

Now that you have obtained respondent cooperation and determined that the respondent qualifies for the interview, you are ready to begin the main phase of questioning.

Quantitative research studies use a variety of questioning approaches and scales to collect information. Structured questioning approaches are either:

1. stand-alone;
2. in a series;
3. in a string.

Stand-alone questions are simply isolated questions or questions that don't connect to a thought pattern. Here are some examples of stand-alone questions:

What one brand of gasoline do you purchase most often?

When you think of brands of gasoline, what are all the brands you can think of?

The last time you bought gasoline, did you purchase other products at the gas station?

How knowledgeable are you when it comes to the mechanics of keeping your car running?

Questioning in a series might best be referred to as branching questions. When a respondent answers a question a certain way, it triggers the next question – or the branch. The branch question is only asked as a result of the answer given to an initial question.

Question 1a below has two branch questions. Questions 1b and 1c are the branch questions and would only be asked if the answer to 1a were YES; otherwise the respondent is skipped to the next question:

1a. In the last 30 days have you seen advertising for discount stores?
   – Yes.
   – No. IF NO, SKIP TO QUESTION 2.

1b. Which of the following discount stores have you seen advertised most often?
   – Costco.
   – Sam's Club.
   – Sears.
   – Target.
   – Wal-Mart.
   – Other.

1c. Where did you see advertising for [mention store shopped in Question 1b]?

- TV.
- Newspaper ad.
- Flyer in mail.
- Radio.
- Other.

Questioning in question strings is a frequently used approach. Here are some examples of question strings:

I am going to read you a series of statements about buying from a catalog. Please indicate whether you agree or disagree with each statement. HERE THE STRING OF STATEMENTS WOULD BE READ BY THE INTERVIEWER ONE AT A TIME.
- Buying from catalogs is fun.
- Buying from catalogs usually saves me money.
- It is more convenient buying from catalogs than going to a retail store.
- You can find unique products when buying from catalogs.
- It is difficult to return products when you buy from catalogs.

Here is another example of a string question:

I am going to read you a list of statements about catalog companies. Please indicate how important or unimportant each is in determining the catalog companies that you purchase from:
- They provide free returns.
- You can easily contact them with questions.
- They carry products that you can't find elsewhere.
- Their products are always in stock.
- Their products are the highest quality.

A string question can list dozens of statements, attributes, or characteristics. Usually each statement can be read by the interviewer and answered in about 10 to 15 seconds. A 25-statement string question can usually be completed in five minutes or less, which makes it a very fast technique for generating information about many issues.

Open-ended questioning

In addition to structured questioning, quantitative surveys may contain open-ended questioning. Open-ended questions are unstructured and do not anticipate a particular response. They allow respondents to use their own words when answering a question. The following are examples of open-ended questioning:

1a. Do you recall seeing advertising for Wal-Mart?
   – Yes. ASK QUESTION 1b.
   – No. SKIP TO QUESTION 2.
1b. What do you recall that Wal-Mart's advertising said or showed?

Comment: The interviewer would record the respondent's response exactly as expressed.
   Another example is:

1a. Have you purchased from catalogs in the past 30 days?
   – Yes. ASK QUESTIONS 1b AND 1c.
   – No. SKIP TO QUESTION 2a.

1b. What do you feel are all the advantages, if any, of purchasing from catalogs?

Comment: The interviewer would record the respondent's response exactly as expressed.

1c. What do you feel are all the disadvantages, if any, of purchasing from catalogs?

Comment: The interviewer would record the respondent's response exactly as expressed.

2a. How would you rate purchasing from catalogs? Do you think it's:
   – An excellent way to buy products
   – A good way
   – A fair way
   – A poor way to buy products

2b. Tell me why you said purchasing from catalogs is [insert answer from question 2a].

Comment: The interviewer would record the respondent's response exactly as expressed.
   As respondents answer open-ended questions, interviewers record their comments verbatim. The main goal of open-ended questions is to allow information to surface that might not be addressed in structured questions.

When you ask open-ended questions, a person called a "coder" must read each answer and code the response(s) into answer categories. That is, each response is put into a category that captures the essence of the remark. The codes are then tabulated and the percentages of respondents giving particular answers are reported.

Scales

Scales are the main tool used in survey questionnaires to collect information. Scales gauge the degree to which an opinion is held or the extent to which respondents have feelings one way or the other about an issue.

Attitudes held by consumers are rarely all positive or all negative. There are many scales at your disposal that measure not only the most positive or most negative attitudes that are held, but also assess the shades of gray that exist.

Scales should be balanced. That is, they should evenly represent both positive and negative attitudes. Consider this question and the scale:

How do you like this chapter of *Guerrilla Marketing Research*? Do you:
- Like it very much
- Like it somewhat
- Neither like nor dislike it
- Dislike it somewhat
- Dislike it very much

The response options are evenly balanced and unbiased. Respondents can choose a totally positive or negative response as well as a positive leaning or a negative leaning. There is also a middle option if the respondent simply doesn't have an opinion.

Consider the question posed another way:

How do you like this chapter of *Guerrilla Marketing Research*? Do you:
- Like it very much
- Like it somewhat
- Like it a little
- Dislike it a little
- Dislike it a lot

There is a decidedly positive bias to these response options. There are three positive and only two negative response options. Even the response "Dislike it a little" has a biased positive tone.

Take another question:

> Think about the last time you flew in a plane. Would you rate the carrier you flew as being:
> – Excellent
> – Good
> – Fair
> – Poor

The four response options represent equanimity. There is neither a positive nor a negative bias. Look at the scale used below:

> Think about the last time you flew in a plane. Would you rate the carrier you flew as being:
> – Excellent
> – Very good
> – Good
> – Fair

Clearly, these responses pose a positive bias. Even the "Fair" response suggests that not all is bad.

There are a number of popular scales used in survey research that are unbiased. Scales are referred to as 4- or 5-point scales. Four-point scales force respondents into leaning one way or the other on a question. Five-point scales provide respondents with a middle ground.

Here is a 4-point agreement scale. In this case, the question is:

> To what extent do you agree with the statement that you enjoy life to its fullest. Do you:
> 1. Agree strongly
> 2. Agree somewhat
> 3. Disagree somewhat
> 4. Disagree strongly

Using a 5-point scale, you would have the same response option plus a middle ground, as follows:

> 1. Agree strongly
> 2. Agree somewhat
> 3. Neither agree nor disagree
> 4. Disagree somewhat
> 5. Disagree strongly

Whether you use a 4- or 5-point scale is usually one of personal choice. One school of thought says that consumers usually lean one way or the other no matter what the question, so a 4-point scale that forces them into a direction is the best. Others say it is equally legitimate for respondents not to have an opinion and therefore providing a mid-point is the best way to go.

Often it will depend on whom you are surveying and the nature of your questions. If you feel your target respondents are unlikely to have an opinion, as might be the case when you are interviewing respondents who may know very little about the subject, go with the 5-point scale. If you are interviewing past customers who have had some experience with your company and products and are likely to have opinions, you might go with a 4-point scale.

Consistency is what is ultimately important. You shouldn't have a 4-point scale for some respondent targets and a 5-point scale for others. This would make it impossible to compare findings across the targets.

Also, if you have a questionnaire with a number of questioning strings, it is usually best to stick to one scale; otherwise respondents tend to become confused going back and forth from a 4-point scale to a 5-point scale or vice versa.

Here are some additional 4- or 5-point scales, all of which are unbiased and, depending upon your questions, are good options for your questionnaire.

A *4-point importance scale*:

- Extremely important.
- Somewhat important.
- Not very important.
- Not at all important.

A *5-point importance scale*:

- Extremely important.
- Somewhat important.
- Neither important nor unimportant.
- Not very important.
- Not at all important.

A *4-point liking scale*:

- Like very much.
- Like somewhat.
- Dislike somewhat.
- Dislike very much.

A *5-point liking scale*:

- Like very much.
- Like somewhat.
- Neither like nor dislike.
- Dislike somewhat.
- Dislike very much.

A *4-point satisfaction scale*:

- Completely satisfied.
- Somewhat satisfied.
- Somewhat dissatisfied.
- Completely dissatisfied.

A *5-point satisfaction scale*:

- Completely satisfied.
- Somewhat satisfied.
- Neither satisfied nor dissatisfied.
- Somewhat dissatisfied.
- Completely dissatisfied.

A *4-point purchase scale*:

- Definitely would purchase.
- Probably would purchase.
- Probably would not purchase.
- Definitely would not purchase.

A *5-point purchase scale*:

- Definitely would purchase.
- Probably would purchase.
- Might or might not purchase.
- Probably would not purchase.
- Definitely would not purchase.

Anchor scales are another popular approach to scaling. Anchor scales, as the name implies, use a top and bottom word or phrase to anchor the scale. Here, respondents are read both ends of the scale and asked to choose the number best describing their attitude. The question here would be:

On a 5-point scale with 5 being "Definitely would purchase" and 1 being "Definitely would not purchase," what number between 5 and 1 best describes your likelihood of purchasing from the Apex catalog?

Definitely would purchase 5 4 3 2 1 Definitely would not purchase

Researchers like anchor scales because they don't have to worry about whether the mid-points of a scale represent a fair balance. For example, the wording "Probably would purchase" might have a different implication to one respondent than it has to another. Using an anchor scale with only the most positive and most negative points expressed eliminates the vagueness of mid-point wording.

Anchor scales are particularly valuable when it is difficult to write a balanced scale. For example, it is difficult to write a balanced scale when evaluating product sweetness. Assume you were judging the taste of a new candy bar and you wanted to evaluate the level of sweetness. With the question "How would you rate the sweetness of the candy bar you tasted?," a 5-point balanced scale might use the words:

1. Much too sweet.
2. A little too sweet.
3. Just about right.
4. Not quite sweet enough.
5. Not at all sweet enough.

An anchor scale might be:

Much too sweet 5 4 3 2 1 Not at all sweet enough

As you can see, both scales evaluate sweetness but come at it differently. If using the wording "A little too sweet" or "Not quite sweet enough" in the balanced scale provides clear direction, use that approach. The wording, though, might have different meanings to your R&D people, who are working to get the right levels of sweetness. In this case, the anchor scale might be easier to interpret.

Another good use of anchor scales is when you are looking for more subtle levels of difference. Assume that you want to evaluate consumer attitudes toward Home Depot and Lowe's on the issue of price. Take the question "Please indicate the number that best describes your attitudes toward the way Home Depot and Lowe's price their products."

You could use a 5-, 7- or 9-point anchor scale, like those illustrated in Table 12.1.

Table 12.1 Anchor scales

5-point:		
Home Depot prices are extremely high	5 4 3 2 1	Home Depot prices are extremely low
Lowe's prices are extremely high	5 4 3 2 1	Lowe's prices are extremely low
7-point:		
Home Depot prices are extremely high	7 6 5 4 3 2 1	Home Depot prices are extremely low
Lowe's prices are extremely high	7 6 5 4 3 2 1	Lowe's prices are extremely low
9-point:		
Home Depot prices are extremely high	9 8 7 6 5 4 3 2 1	Home Depot prices are extremely low
Lowe's prices are extremely high	9 8 7 6 5 4 3 2 1	Lowe's prices are extremely low

All three scales can be used effectively to evaluate attitudes toward price. But because of the additional number of rating points on the 7- and 9-point scales, there is a greater opportunity to observe subtle differences that might exist.

Overall, when choosing scales to use in your questionnaire, keep the following in mind:

- Deciding on a particular scale is more often a matter of personal preference than scientific principle.
- Once you have chosen a particular scale, you should be consistent and stick with it. If you want comparative data from target to target and from study to study, you must keep the scales constant.
- Sometimes it's impossible to create a scale that is totally balanced or in which the anchors represent both ends precisely.

If your scale has a positive or negative bias, using the scale over and over again from study to study will at least produce a constant bias. You'll be interpreting the data from the same points of view, which is always the goal anyway.

Developing the main body of your questionnaire

There are a number of important things to keep in mind as you write a questionnaire. They are:

- If respondents become aware of the study sponsor it may present a positive or negative influence in the way they answer subsequent questions. Carefully consider if or when you reveal the sponsor.
- If unaided questions are important, do not give clues as to the study sponsor until after such questions are asked.
- Questionnaire flow is usually from the more general to the more specific.
- Demographic questions and other "sensitive" questions should be asked at the end of the questionnaire.

Sponsor awareness

Earlier, I talked about gaining the cooperation of respondents by informing them of the study sponsor. This is appropriate when you are conducting studies in which:

- The nature of the study isn't such that mentioning the sponsor might bias answers either positively or negatively. If you are conducting a satisfaction study among your own customers, for example, respondents are more likely to give honest, straightforward opinions when they know you are the study sponsor. Not knowing the sponsor makes them suspicious and less cooperative.
- You are evaluating new products, services, or ideas and the company or brand would be an important part of potential success or failure of the effort.
- The subject matter is highly sensitive, and respondents might not be totally forthcoming without knowing who is using the information.

For most research studies, the information being collected dictates that respondents be kept in the dark about the sponsor, at least for a portion of the interview. These studies include:

- when you want top-of-mind spontaneous responses to questions (e.g., "When you think of makes of automobiles, what is the first name that comes to mind?" or "Please tell me the names of all the banks you can think of in your community");
- when you are comparing your company, brand or product to one or more competitors;
- when you feel that knowledge of the sponsor up front might bias the respondent either positively or negatively (e.g., your company did something that was in the news and mention of it might stimulate comments that wouldn't otherwise surface).

Unaided questions

Survey questionnaires may feature a series of questions regarding company awareness, attitude, or image. In this case, asking questions in an unaided manner is important. "Unaided" simply means that the respondent has not been provided with any information by the interviewer that would help him or her answer the question. Consider the following unaided questions:

What are the names of all the places you can think of that sell home improvement products?

What are the names of all the places that sell home improvement products that you have seen advertised in the past 30 days?

What one place that sells home improvement products do you feel gives you the best value for your money?

What one place that sells home improvement products do you shop at most often?

Considering all the home improvement stores you shop at, approximately how much do you spend per year at each?

What are the most important reasons you chose to shop at one home improvement store over another?

Conversely, aided questions are also important. "Aided" questioning means that the interviewer has given the respondent information to answer the question. Consider several of the previous unaided questions and their aided counterparts:

Unaided: What are the names of all the places you can think of that sell home improvement products? DO NOT READ LIST. CHECK ALL THAT ARE MENTIONED.
- Ace Hardware   _____
- Home Depot   _____
- Lowe's   _____
- Menard's   _____
- Tru-Value Hardware   _____
- Other mentions (WRITE IN)

Aided: FOR ALL THE PLACES NOT MENTIONED IN THE UNAIDED QUESTION, THE INTERVIEWER WOULD ASK THE RESPONDENT: In the past 30 days, have you seen or heard advertising for any of the following?

– Ace Hardware	Yes __	No __
– Home Depot	Yes __	No __
– Lowe's	Yes __	No __
– Menard's	Yes __	No __
– Tru-Value Hardware	Yes __	No __

Unaided: For all the home improvement places you shop at, approximately how much do you spend per year at each? DO NOT READ LIST. CHECK ALL THAT ARE MENTIONED.

- Ace Hardware _____
- Home Depot _____
- Lowe's _____
- Menard's _____
- Tru-Value Hardware _____
- Other mentions (WRITE IN)

Aided: FOR THOSE PLACES WHERE NO SPENDING WAS MENTIONED IN UNAIDED QUESTIONING, THE INTERVIEWER WOULD ASK THE RESPONDENT: In the past year, how much have you spent at any of the following?

- Ace Hardware _____
- Home Depot _____
- Lowe's _____
- Menard's _____
- Tru-Value Hardware _____
- Other mentions (WRITE IN)

Unaided recall is usually regarded as a stronger indication of share of the consumer's mind than is aided recall. But simply because a respondent fails to mention a company, brand, or product when asked unaided, it does not suggest that the respondent holds it in less esteem. Aided recall triggers additional recall. *Taken together, unaided and aided questioning provide a more complete picture of respondent awareness, attitudes, and behavior.*

Phrasing questions

When phrasing questions, follow the guidelines below.

Avoid biased phrasing at all costs

Consider the question "What do you like about driving a car?" There is a built-in assumption in the question that the respondent will like something about driving a car. When asked this way, it tends to force respondents to mention something they like.

Consider the question written in an unbiased manner: "What, if anything, do you like about driving a car?" By simply using "if anything" as part of the question phrasing, the respondent is not put on the spot to find something to like.

Here are other examples of biased and unbiased questions:

Biased: There are many factors that are important when buying over the internet. Tell me which ones you feel are most important.

This assumes that there are factors that are important.

Unbiased: There are many factors that may or may not be important to you when buying over the internet. Tell me which, if any, you feel are most important.

Biased: How often do you just hang up without listening when somebody calls you on the telephone and tries to sell you something?

This assumes the respondent will hang up.

Unbiased: Consider the last 10 times somebody might have called you on the telephone and tried to sell you something. How many times out of 10 would you say you've just hung up on the person calling without listening?

Biased: The last time you shopped for groceries, which soft drink brands did you purchase for your home?

This assumes soft drinks were purchased on the last shopping trip.

Unbiased: The last time you purchased soft drinks for your home, which brands did you buy?

When phrasing questions, don't assume that the respondent holds particular attitudes or behaves in a certain way.

Keep questions or statements to a single thought

A dual-thought question would be "What, if anything, do you like or dislike about your dentist?" With such a question, respondents tend to focus first on the strongest likes or dislikes. If it happens to be something they like, they will give less thought to what they might dislike, and vice versa.

If would be better to split this into two questions, one focusing only on likes and the other on dislikes.

String questions are easy to write with multiple thoughts and, therefore, can be problematic. Consider this string question:

> I am going to read you a list of statements that describe what people look for when they choose a bank. Please tell me how important or unimportant each is to you.

> The bank should have friendly and knowledgeable people.

Friendly is one thought; knowledgeable is another thought.

> The bank should be open long hours and at night.

Long hours is one thought; open at night is a second thought.

> The bank should offer extra services such as being able to buy and sell stocks or being able to buy life insurance.

Buy and sell stocks is one thought; buying life insurance is a second thought.

> The bank should offer free postage when I want to bank by mail as well as free internet banking.

Free postage is one thought; free internet banking is a second thought.

When you ask a dual-thought question, you are stuck with interpreting both issues as one. It's probably a good idea that a bank should have both friendly and knowledgeable people, but it may not be necessary. Being just the friendliest bank could set it apart, as could just being the bank with the most knowledgeable people.

Phrase questions as directly as possible

Questions should be precise and to the point. They should not be wordy or verbose. If it takes you more than two sentences for an interviewer to pose your question, it's probably too long. Here is a ridiculous and real example of a question from a telephone questionnaire:

> The following statements I am going to read to you deal with attitudes you may have toward buying from catalogs. In this sense, we mean buying from a catalog where you have mailed or telephoned in your order and your merchandise was delivered to your home, office, or elsewhere, or by some type of delivery service. We do not mean where you may have ordered by mail or phone and then gone to a retail store or outlet to pick up the merchandise yourself. For each statement please tell me how much you agree or disagree that the statement describes how you feel about buying from catalogs.
>
> Let's use a 5-point scale where "5" means you agree strongly that the statement describes how you feel about purchasing merchandise through a catalog and "1" means that you disagree strongly that the statement describes how you feel about purchasing merchandise through a catalog.
>
> Of course, you may use any number in between, depending on how much you agree or disagree that the statement describes how you feel about buying from catalogs.

The question could be more succinctly phrased as follows:

> I am going to read you some statements about buying from catalogs where your order is delivered to your home or office. Each statement can be rated on a 5-point scale with "5" meaning you agree strongly with the statement and "1" meaning you disagree strongly.

Here is another overly wordy question:

> People can describe companies many different ways. There are different words and phrases that are more commonly used than others. Some are positive, some neutral, and some negative. I am going to read you the names of several companies, one at a time, and then read words and phrases to describe that company. After each word or phrase, simply say "yes" if you feel it describes the company and "no" if you feel it doesn't describe the company.

This question could be easily pared down:

I am going to give you the names of several companies. Simply say "yes" or "no" if you think the words or phrases I read describe that company.

Keep in mind that respondents can have difficulty remembering or understanding long and involved questions. While you might think that length is important to asking a question, short and simple usually works just as well.

Self-administered questionnaires

Most self-administered questionnaires arrive by mail or via the internet. On occasion, they may be handed out.

Questionnaires that are filled out by the respondent without interviewer assistance should follow many of the same guidelines previously discussed. But there are other issues to consider when writing self-administered questionnaires, as set out below.

Simplicity, simplicity and simplicity

It is very easy for respondents to become confused when filling out a questionnaire. To cut down on confusion, follow these guidelines:

1. The main instructions for completing the questionnaire should make the task seem effortless (e.g., "The questions in this survey can be answered by simply placing an 'X' where indicated. Be sure to answer each question. Don't skip any questions. Thank you for your time").
2. Use at least 12-point typeface to enhance readability.
3. Use bold type and/or underline to highlight important elements in a question (e.g., "How many times have you purchased from a **retail store** in the past **30** days?").
4. Put at least one line between questions.
5. Don't have questions that bleed from one page to another.

Reduce question skipping

Don't jump respondents around. Keep questions in sequential order. As much as possible, one question should follow the next. Believe it or not, up to 20 percent of respondents will fail to read or follow an instruction that tells them to skip from question 1 to question 3.

There are times when the answer to one question must dictate the next question to answer. If you have to skip respondents, assume that a child is filling out the questionnaire. The following example illustrates this mentality:

1a. Have you ever gone to a flea market?
  – Yes   _____
  IF YES, ANSWER QUESTION 1b.
  – No   _____
  IF NO, GO TO QUESTION 2.

1b. IF YES TO 1a. How often do you go to flea markets? (**Check one line only**.)
  – Once a week or more often   _____
  – Two to three times per month   _____
  – Once a month or more   _____

Provide an instruction for each question

Each and every question should tell respondents exactly what you want them to do. See these examples:

Example 1
1. Put an "X" next to the one statement below that best describes you. (**Place an "X" on <u>one</u> line only.**)
  – I'm an avid collector   _____
  – I only have a passing interest in collecting anything   _____
  – I don't collect anything   _____

Example 2
1a. In the past 12 months, how many times have you purchased a gift? (**Place an "X" on <u>one</u> line only below in column 1a.**)

1b. In the past 12 months, how many times have you purchased a gift from a discount store? (**Place an "X" on <u>one</u> line only below under in column 1b.**)

	Question 1a Gift purchase	Question 1b Discount store
Have not purchased a gift	___	___
Purchased 1 time	___	___
Purchased 2 or more times	___	___

Example 3

1. Listed below are statements about purchasing gifts. For each statement, place an "X" on the one line that describes the extent to which you agree or disagree with the statement. (**Remember to "X" one answer for <u>each</u> statement.**)

	Agree strongly	Agree somewhat	Disagree somewhat	Disagree strongly
You always look for unique gifts	—	—	—	—
You like nostalgic gifts	—	—	—	—
You like to give high-quality gifts	—	—	—	—
You like to give art as gifts	—	—	—	—

Avoid open-ended questions

In a self-administered questionnaire, if respondents even write a response to an open-ended essay question, they won't provide more than superficial comments. Questions like "Why do you like visiting Mexico?" or "Write down your last experience of visiting Mexico" will generate little more than one- or two-word answers. Spending money to tabulate such responses is rarely worth the effort.

Questions in self-administered questionnaires should be 100 percent structured. All the respondent should have to do is check a pre-listed answer.

If you think you have to ask a "Why?" or essay-type question, you haven't done your homework or are being lazy. The fact is that you should know the responses you want to quantify *before* you collect data using a self-administered questionnaire.

Consider the issue of questionnaire control

You have no control over what respondents will do before they fill out a self-administered questionnaire. They may first read it over completely. In doing so, they will become aware of the issues your questioning is addressing, which could influence how they respond. They might also fill it out over a couple of days with those issues in mind.

Think about lack of control. If you think a question might possibly be misinterpreted, assume it will be and rewrite it. If you feel that answering certain questions first might affect how respondents answer subsequent questions, you are probably right. Reconsider the order. If confidentiality is important, you should make sure that you are hiding the study sponsor as best you can.

Questionnaire length versus clarity

First and foremost, motivating the respondent to complete a self-administered questionnaire, no matter what the length, is job number one. Gaining respondent cooperation is discussed in detail in Chapter 14, "How to conduct surveys."

Suffice it to say, respondents will fill out a 40-page self-administered questionnaire if it is well written, easy to complete, and interesting. They will toss a two-page questionnaire away if it is cluttered and complex.

Question context for interviewer and self-administered questionnaires

The art of developing an effective questionnaire lies in the context in which you pose a question. Context is the point of view the question presents. Here are several different questioning contexts or points of view for generating unaided awareness of places that sell clothing:

When you think of buying clothing for yourself, what places come to mind?

When you think about places that sell upscale clothing for yourself, what places come to mind?

When you think about places that sell upscale clothing for yourself by catalog or the internet, what places come to mind?

Each of the above questions provides a different context and could generate different answers. The first context is very general – only about places to buy clothes. The second narrows the context to upscale clothing. The third is even more narrow yet, referring to upscale clothing via catalogs or the internet.

When writing questions, it is very important that the context of the questions be clear to you. You must be convinced the question will give you information that is in the context you seek. The worst feeling in the world is looking at how respondents have answered and realizing that the question is irrelevant because you have not posed it in the right context.

The contextual questions in the following sections are provided as guidelines for writing a questionnaire. They should be helpful when writing questions that deal with a variety of topics. Use them as you deem appropriate.

Notes of clarification: The following contextual questions are written to reflect companies that sell retail-oriented products. When it comes to financial companies, professional services firms, or other organizations selling non-retail-type products or services, the wording of the questions should be altered to reflect the marketplace. That is, consumers don't buy checking accounts; they choose a place to open a checking account. Executives don't buy accounting firms; they choose an accounting firm, etc.

The questioning contexts that are illustrated are most appropriate for interviewer-administered questionnaires. In self-administered questionnaires, in which response options are shown as part of the question, you could not, for example, consider answers to be unaided. If you are writing a self-administered questionnaire, the questioning contexts should be altered to reflect the previously discussed self-administered questionnaire guidelines.

Generating top-of-mind unaided responses

For brand awareness:

> When you think of [insert your product category], what is the first [insert brand/company/product type] that comes to mind?
> What other [insert brands/companies/product types] come to mind?

For advertising awareness:

> When you think of [insert your product category], in the past [30 days or whatever time frame is appropriate], what is the one [insert brand/company/product type] that you have seen advertised most often?
> What other [insert brands/companies/product types] have you seen advertised in the past [30 days or whatever time frame is appropriate]?

For brand loyalty:

> When you buy [insert your product category], what one [insert brand/company/product type] do you buy most often?
> What other [insert brands/companies/product types] do you buy from?

For brand attrition:

> What [insert brands/companies/product types] would you not consider buying?

The above brand loyalty and brand attrition unaided questions should include a list of brands, companies or product types so that the interviewer can "X" the answers rather than writing in responses.

Generating top-of-mind aided responses

Note: Top-of-mind aided response questioning is appropriate for both interviewer-administered and self-administered questionnaires.
   For brand awareness:

I am going to mention a list of [insert brands/companies/product types] one at a time. After I read each, tell me if you have heard of it.

For advertising awareness:

I am going to mention a list of [insert brands/companies/product types] one at a time. After I read each, tell me if you have heard of it or seen it advertised in the past [30 days or whatever time frame is appropriate].

For brand loyalty:

When you buy [insert brands/companies/product types], have you purchased any of the following [read the brands/companies/product types one at a time] in the past [30 days or whatever time frame is appropriate]?

For brand attrition:

For each of the following [insert brands/companies/product types] that I read, which, if any, would you not consider buying?

When generating aided awareness, the interviewer should mention only names that were not previously chosen or marked with an "X" when asking the question unaided.
   The following context questions are written for a string series of statements.

Note of clarification: Five-point scales are used in the context questions below. Other scales are equally appropriate, e.g., 7-, 9-, or 10-point scales. Please refer to the scale section earlier in this chapter for additional options.

Generating importance

When you want to determine how important a number of characteristics are to purchases, use the following context question:

I am going to read you a list of statements regarding [insert product category]. For each statement, how important or unimportant is it to you when it comes to buying [insert product category]? A "5" would mean it is extremely important, a "1" not at all important, or you can rate it any number in between. The first statement is [insert statement].

Generating agreement

When you want to determine whether respondents agree or disagree with statements regarding your products or your competitors' products, use the following context question:

I am going to read you a list of statements regarding [insert product category] and I would like to know the extent to which you agree or disagree with each. A "5" would mean that you agree strongly with the statement, a "1" means that you disagree strongly with the statement, or you can rate it any number in between. The first statement is [insert statement].

Generating company or brand profiles

When you want to determine profiles of companies or brands on a series of statements, use the following context question:

I am going to read you a list of statements regarding [insert the company/ brand]. For each statement, please tell me the extent to which you agree or disagree that the statement describes the [company/brand]. A "5" means you agree strongly that it describes the [company/brand], a "1" means you disagree strongly that it describes the [company/brand], or you can rate it any number in between. The first statement is [insert statement].

Generating overall attitude

In almost any survey, there should be an overall attitude question – one that captures the respondent's *summary* feeling about the company, brand, or product. Overall attitude is often used as a dependent variable when analyzing data (the use of a dependent variable is explained further in Chapter 17).

Consider the following context questions for generating overall attitude:

Taking everything you think into consideration, would you rate [insert the brand/company/product] as being:

- Superior   _____
- Excellent   _____
- Good   _____
- Fair   _____
- Poor   _____

Taking everything you think into consideration, how would you rate [insert the brand/company/product] on a 9-point scale? A "9" would be the best, "1" would be the worst, or you could rate it anywhere in between.

Note of clarification: The scales used on the context question above can be changed to a 7- or 5-point scale, as you deem appropriate.

In the future, how likely would you be to purchase [insert the brand/company/product]:
- Definitely would purchase   _____
- Probably would purchase   _____
- Might or might not purchase   _____
- Probably would not purchase   _____
- Definitely would not purchase   _____

Anchor questions

Anchor questions are particularly appropriate when generating company or brand profiles and when evaluating reactions to products. Anchor questions are more easily answered when respondents can see the question and "X" a response. The context examples below illustrate this. Of course, you should insert the words or phrases that are appropriate to your brand, company, or product.

Listed below are word pairs with opposite meanings. For each pair, please place an "X" on the line that comes closest to the word that you feel describes [insert the brand, company, or product]. Be sure to mark an "X" a line for each pair.

	5	4	3	2	1	
Exciting	__	__	__	__	__	Boring
Contemporary	__	__	__	__	__	Old-fashioned
Unique	__	__	__	__	__	Common
Friendly	__	__	__	__	__	Impersonal
Fun	__	__	__	__	__	Dull
Classic	__	__	__	__	__	Trendy

Note of clarification: When administering anchor questions by phone, you can use telephone-type wording (e.g., "You would choose a '5' if you felt that the company was *exciting*, a '1' if you thought it was *boring*, or you can use any number in between"). Also consider using scales that have only two anchor points, as follows:

> When thinking about [insert the brand/company/product], would you say it was:
>
> More exciting brand _____ or More dull brand _____
>
> More contemporary brand _____ or More old-fashioned brand _____
>
> More unique brand _____or More common brand _____

Forced-choice questions

If you are comparing two or more alternatives and you want to determine whether there is a clear winner, forced-choice questions should be considered (i.e., when comparing products, ads, promotions, premiums, etc.). Here are several examples of context questions in forced-choice situations:

> Please look at both of these premiums that you would get free if you purchased a new brand of coffee you had not tried in the past. Which one would most likely cause you to purchase the new brand?
> – Premium #1 _____
> – Premium #2 _____
>
> A new flavored cola drink is coming on the market. It could come in three flavors. Which one flavor would you most likely buy first?
> – Chocolate _____
> – Lemon   _____
> – Cherry   _____
>
> Here are two advertisements for Sears. Please read both and choose the one that you find most believable about what is being said.
> – Ad #1 _____
> – Ad #2 _____

Price

There are many questions that you can ask to determine how much consumers will spend on a product. The problem with pricing questions is that if you ask respondents a direct price question their answers usually over- or underestimate reality.

Take the question "How much would you be willing to spend for a new computer?" Whatever answer you give might be totally unrealistic compared to the actual price you would have to pay given your needs.

It is always better to put pricing questions in a context. If you were trying to determine how much a person would be willing to spend for a weekend night at a luxury hotel, you could frame the question as follows:

> Luxury hotel rooms vary in price. During the week you could spend as little as $200 for a luxury hotel room or as much as $600 for a five-star, top-of-the-line hotel. If you wanted to spend a weekend night at a luxury hotel, how much would you be willing to spend?
> Record amount: _____

Another way to determine the price of a luxury hotel room would be using a scale approach. Here's an example:

> Luxury hotel rooms vary in price. During the week, you could spend as little as $200 for a luxury hotel room or as much as $600 for a five-star, top-of-the-line hotel. If you wanted to spend a weekend night at a luxury hotel, would you be willing to spend $200?
> – Yes _____
> – No _____

If yes, ask the respondent if he or she would be willing to spend $225. If yes, ask if he or she would be willing to spend $250, and continue higher in $25 increments until the respondent is unwilling to go higher.

If no, ask if the respondent would be willing to spend $175. If no, ask if he or she would be willing to spend $150, and continue lower in $25 increments until the respondent gives a "yes" answer.

The up/down scale approach to determining price is popular. It sets a realistic context at the outset and then tests the respondent's tolerance for paying more or less. Remember, with pricing questions, the closer you can get to describing your products and benefits, i.e., setting a realistic context, the closer you'll come to getting the real price that consumers are willing to pay.

But I would caution that, if your *prime* research objective is to determine the price that consumers will pay for your product or service, and if the success of your company hinges on getting good results, you should hire a research professional. *Getting a realistic assessment of what consumers will pay is one of the most difficult tasks in survey research and not an area for novice Guerrilla researchers.*

Questionnaire flow

Questionnaires have a flow to them. Following the screening phase, a questionnaire usually flows from the general to the specific. But because the types of studies you can do vary so greatly, as do the goals of every questionnaire, there are no hard-and-fast rules for the flow or sequence in which questions should be asked. Nevertheless, I would suggest following certain guidelines:

- *Keep the respondent in one mindset at a time.* If at all possible, complete all your questions about a topic before moving on. For example, don't ask about a favorite place to shop, then about brands used and then go back to additional questioning on a favorite place to shop.
- *Ask the easy questions first.* Simple questions regarding behavior, such as frequency of buying, brands purchased, or places shopped at, are easy for respondents to answer because these don't require a lot of thinking or pondering. Because of this, respondents quickly get comfortable with the interview.
- *More involved or introspective questions should be asked after the easier questions.* Be prepared to transition to questions that require thought and consideration after only a few minutes of the interview, once the easy questions are out of the way. Respondents don't mind giving more thought to complex questions once they are comfortable with the interview process.
- *If it's important to tell respondents who the study is for, do so at the last possible moment.* Sometimes you'll have to identify the sponsor at the beginning, but when this isn't necessary keep the respondent in the dark. Once respondents know who is doing the research, every answer they give will be with that knowledge and will present an informed bias.
- *Save sensitive questions for the end.* Again, this might not always be possible, but, when it doesn't matter, be aware that sensitive questions can alienate respondents and turn them off to the entire interview process.

THE DEMOGRAPHIC PHASE

Demographic questions such as age, occupation, number of children, income, and other sensitive personal questions should be asked at the end of the interview. Respondents are far more likely to give personal information after they have achieved a certain level of rapport with the interviewer and the interview is about to end. When asking demographic questions, ask such questions in generalities rather than in *specifics*. The following are examples:

General: Is your age (READ CATEGORIES):
- Under 21 _____
- 21 to 34 _____
- 35 to 44 _____
- 45 to 54 _____
- 55 to 64 _____
- 65 or older _____

Specific: Tell me your age. _____

General: Is your yearly family income (READ CATEGORIES):
- Under $25,000 _____
- $25,000 to $49,000 _____
- $50,000 to $74,999 _____
- $75,000 to $99,999 _____
- $100,000 or more _____

Specific: What is your yearly household income? _____

General: How many children do you have living at home? Do you have (READ CATEGORIES):
- None _____
- One _____
- Two to three _____
- Four or more _____

Specific: Tell me how many children you have living at home. _____

While it may be necessary to ask certain demographic questions in the screening phase, only those that are absolutely necessary to determine if the respondent qualifies for the interview should be asked at that time.

THE THANK-YOU PHASE

Telephone solicitation by telemarketers has hurt the market research industry and caused many people to be reluctant to cooperate with well-meaning market researchers. The American Marketing Association views it as highly unethical when a respondent is solicited to buy something under the guise of completing a market research interview. Therefore, when thanking respondents for their time and cooperation it helps the credibility of the research profession to reiterate that respondent opinions will indeed remain confidential and that no one will contact respondents as a result of their cooperation.

13

Sampling

Exit surveys and polls were certainly ubiquitous in the 2004 U.S. Presidential election. One exit survey reported that the candidate's moral character was the major factor in determining voter choice, as shown in Table 13.1.

What nonsense. There isn't an attitude survey in the world that doesn't have an *error range* associated with each number, that is, the range that exists around each number indicating that, if the study were repeated, the number could vary upward or downward in that range.

In this case, much was made of the factor of moral character as the chief determinant in why George W. Bush was reelected.

The error range surrounding this study was +/–4 percent. That means that, if the study were conducted again, all the numbers could vary either higher or lower by as much as four percentage points. The moral character figure of 22 percent could go as low as 18 percent while the war in Iraq

Table 13.1   Voter choice issues

Major issue in determining voter choice	Percentage choosing
Moral character	22
The economy	21
Domestic issues	19
The war in Iraq	18
Other issues	20

figure could go as high as 22 percent. In a statistical sense, then, there are four equally valid factors that determined voter choice, and focusing on only one factor as the prime reason for voter choice is a distortion of the facts.

SAMPLING AND ERROR RANGE

The theory of sampling is quite simple. If you interview 300 people, you want to be confident that their attitudes are the same as those of the next 300 you interview, and the 300 after that, and so on until you've interviewed everybody there is to be interviewed. This is commonly referred to as "projectability."

Survey research seeks to ensure that a small sample of people will give you the same answers you'd get if you expanded the sample size and interviewed a far greater number.

Start noticing the sample sizes for surveys that are reported in the newspapers or magazines. Most surveys report their results based on sample sizes as small as 400 respondents. Even polling surveys used for predicting how voters will vote rarely exceed 1,000 respondents. The entire basis of statistical theory rests on the idea that, by interviewing a few well-chosen respondents, it is possible to represent the attitudes of the many who were not chosen to be interviewed.

There is an error range around every number generated in every market research survey. Again, that is the range around which a number can vary if the study were undertaken exactly the same way a second time.

Say Bush is leading Kerry 49 percent to 47 percent with a four percentage point margin of error. That simply means that, if the study were repeated again and again until everyone in the United States were asked who they would vote for, the data would not vary by more than four percentage points.

That means that Bush's 49 percent could be as high at 53 percent or as low as 45 percent, and Kerry's 47 percent could be as high as 51 percent and as low at 43 percent – a statistical dead heat, too close to predict the winner. And that's exactly why no one could predict, with absolute certainty, who would win the 2004 election.

In survey research, the margin of error range is always taken into account in order to determine the optimum sample size or the number of respondents that should be interviewed.

Table 13.2 shows the margin of error either higher or lower around given sample sizes.

Table 13.2 Margin of error

Survey sample size	Margin of error %*
2000	2
1500	3
1000	3
900	3
800	3
700	4
600	4
500	4
400	5
300	6
200	7
150	8
100	10
50	14

*assumes a 95% level of confidence

If you look at a sample size of 150, the margin of error is +/–8 percent at the 95 percent confidence level. That means that, if the survey shows that 60 percent of the respondents state that they like the taste of your product and 40 percent say they don't like the taste, there is a statistical difference. With an 8 percent error range, the 60 percent could go no lower than 52 percent and the 40 percent no higher that 48 percent. Therefore, you can be 95 percent confident that in questioning every possible respondent in the end you would find that more people like the taste than dislike the taste.

You should also notice how little the error range decreases as you interview more people. By interviewing 300 respondents instead of 150, the error range only decreases two percentage points, from 8 percent to 6 percent. And by interviewing 400 respondents rather than 300, you only pick up one percentage point.

The reason survey research studies are conducted with relatively small numbers of respondents is because there is usually no justification for spending the extra money to interview more people. The data simply won't be that much more accurate.

A word about levels of confidence

Unfortunately it is never possible to be 100 percent confident that data will fall within the sample size error range. If you conduct the study again, there is always a small chance that something strange will occur and that the data will be off by more than the error range. But for all intents and purposes, being able to read data at a 95 percent level of confidence, where there is only a 5 percent chance the data are erroneous, is good enough.

Interestingly, many researchers and marketers are content to make key decisions if they can be 90 percent or even 80 percent confident in the data.

Think about it this way. If you have to make a decision in which large sums of money are on the line, would you rather make that decision knowing there is only a 5 percent, 10 percent, or 20 percent chance that your decision will be wrong, or would you rather save the money you spend on the research and go with your gut? If you don't like the odds, save your money on survey research.

DETERMINING SAMPLE SIZE

Determining the proper survey sample size for a study revolves around a number of factors. They include:

- *Error-range size.* This is always the biggest shot in the dark. If you are confident that the survey will show big differences in respondent attitude, you could be confident choosing a smaller sample size with a big error range. For example, assume that you are doing a survey to determine the most important attributes in choosing which home improvement store to shop at. Table 13.3 shows a list of attributes on

Table 13.3 Attribute importance example

Attribute	Percentage rating as most important	
	150 sample %	200 sample %
Convenience	80	80
Price	50	50
Selection	45	45
One-stop shopping	35	35
Carries well-known brands	20	20

shopping importance ranked for two sample sizes. It shows that, irrespective of the sample size, the same percentage of respondents chose the same attributes as most important. If you knew going into the study that "Convenience" would so dominate the attributes, you could have chosen to go with the 150 sample size. With an 8 percent error range around the 150 sample, the 80 percent around "Convenience" could go no lower than 72 percent. And if the 50 percent around "Price" went to 58 percent, "Convenience" would still be significantly more important than "Price."

But with a sample size of 150 and an 8 percent error range you could not have concluded that "One-stop shopping" was significantly more important than "Carries well-known brands." Here, the 35 percent could be as low as 27 percent and the 20 percent as high as 28 percent, indicating no statistical difference in the number. With a 7 percent error range around a 200 sample size, though, you would have a statistical difference. Unfortunately, you don't get the luxury of this hindsight when determining your survey sample size.

- *Target markets.* In the above example, the assumption is that only one target market is important: home improvement store shoppers in general. Here, a sample of 150 would be the minimum you'd want to interview. But if you wanted to determine, among home improvement shoppers, whether males have attitudes that are different from those of females, or younger shoppers have attitudes that are different from those of older shoppers, your sample size would have to increase to at least 300. Here, you would want to interview 300 respondents: 150 males and 150 females and, within each of these segments, 75 younger respondents and 75 older respondents. In viewing the data with these sample sizes you could determine with a reasonable degree of statistical accuracy whether there are major differences in the attitudes of each target segment.
- *Cost.* It goes without saying that, the more respondents you interview, the more costly the study. This reality forces priorities and compromises as there is usually a trade-off between what can be afforded and the optimum sample size.

THEORETICAL VERSUS PRACTICAL

There are a voluminous number of books and articles written on how to determine the proper sample size for market research studies. If you are a statistics nut, you can spend hours reading about random stratified sampling as opposed to quota sampling, non-response bias, low response bias, and the dozens of other factors that can play havoc with your study.

When you are through learning all there is to learn about sampling, you'll probably be left shaking your head. What you are likely to conclude is that rigid adherence to scientific sampling principles is impractical. Even if they could be adhered to, you would likely find that the expense of doing so would be ridiculous.

This is not to minimize the importance of understanding good sampling procedures. For the professional researcher, a working knowledge of these influences is essential. The assumption here is that you don't wish to follow a research career or become an expert at sampling, so I will suggest some practical sampling guidelines.

In conducting thousands of surveys, I have established a number of generalities about sample size. They are:

- A minimum sample size of 600 is required for a basic strategy study. This sample will provide flexibility in viewing data across a number of target segments. Rarely will it be necessary for Guerrillas to conduct a study in which the sample size is larger than 1,000. Studies with such large sample sizes are usually undertaken by large companies wishing to understand the attitudes of many different customer and prospect targets.
- A robust sample for most research studies other than a strategy study is 300. Going beyond a sample size of 300 does not generate a lower error range that is worth the added cost.
- Sample sizes of 150 are usually viable for smaller tactical studies such as advertising communications, product, or packaging studies. These are studies in which only two or three alternatives are tested against each other and it is not necessary to view the data from more than one target segment.
- Going below a sample of 100 is risky and, if possible, should be avoided. The error range of +/–10 percent is considered quite large and will only produce a valid statistical difference when there are wide differences in the attitudes and opinions of respondents. When there are relatively subtle differences, a sample size of 100 will not provide data that are statistically significant.

REPRESENTATIVE SAMPLING

What you are trying to accomplish in any sampling procedure is to be confident that the attitudes of the people you interview are the same as the attitudes of the people you don't interview. That means that you do every-thing practical to generate a *representative* sample.

If you send out a mail questionnaire to 10,000 people and 5 percent respond, you have a 500 sample size, which, if looked at in isolation, could be considered a good sample for a survey. But with only a 5 percent response rate, you must question whether your 500 sample is representative. Basic to this is the question of whether the attitudes of the 9,500 who did not respond are the same as those of the 500 who did respond.

With such a small response rate, you are left wondering if those who did respond might have an ax to grind and will tend to be overly negative in their answers. Or it could even be the opposite. Maybe they are particularly positive and will provide overly buoyant responses. They may also be consumers who are atypical demographically and responded because they had nothing better to do.

When conducting telephone surveys, generating a representative sample is also an issue. Say you want to complete 300 telephone interviews, and you have a list of 10,000 phone numbers of people who are likely to qualify for your interview. You will want to ensure that the telephone interview service that you use has a software program that dials those 10,000 numbers in a random sequence. This ensures that all 10,000 have an equal opportunity of being represented in your ending sample of 300.

Good sampling means that every person in your target audience has an equal opportunity of being interviewed. It also mandates that your response rate is high enough to provide confidence that the attitudes of those you don't question are the same as those you do question.

Achieving good response rates

Getting a good representative sample is largely a function of response rate. If only 5 in 100 people (5 percent) agree to answer your questionnaire, whether it's over the phone, by mail, or via the internet, you are likely to have a response bias. If, though, 30 percent, 40 percent, or more agree to be interviewed, you can be far more confident that you have reduced any potential response rate bias.

More people than you might think will give you their opinions if they are approached correctly and there is incentive enough for them to respond.

APPROACHING RESPONDENTS

Previously, I discussed how to approach respondents in order to gain cooperation to be interviewed. In addition to assuring them that no attempt will be made to sell anything and after identifying the sponsor of the study, intangibles such as interviewer tone and getting to respondents at a convenient time are also important. Assuming that you are conducting a telephone study, achieving a random sample is an issue to be discussed with your telephone interviewing service.

It is important to remember that you can motivate almost anybody to respond to a survey if you offer them the right incentive. Usually, that means money.

Here are some guidelines:

- *Telephone.* If your questionnaire is no longer than 30 minutes, a $5 incentive is usually enough to keep a respondent on the line. For longer interviews, incentives should increase proportionately: $10 for 35 minutes, $15 for 40 minutes, and so forth is a good rule of thumb. Remember, though, that the nature of your questioning as well as the type of respondents you are seeking together with the value of their time will influence the amount of the incentive. For example, consumers of high-incidence products and services require smaller incentives than do consumers of low-incidence or professional products and services. When conducting telephone interviews with professionals (owners of companies, lawyers, medical doctors, purchasing agents, etc.), incentives could vary. Start out offering $20 for interviews in excess of 20 minutes but if this proves unsuccessful be ready to go higher. An incentive of $100 is not uncommon when interviewing professionals such as doctors, lawyers, or business executives.

- *Mail studies.* Most studies conducted by mail should have a small incentive included when you mail the questionnaire. I have found that a new $2 bill is great for getting attention and stimulating response. Sometimes you can get by with a $1 bill if the questionnaire is relatively short (two to three pages or four to six sides of questionnaire). Offering an additional incentive to be mailed when the questionnaire is returned also will greatly enhance response. A $5 or $10 bill is common for most studies conducted among consumers. Again, for professionals, your incentive will have to be higher in order to generate a good sample. I have found that, in most cases, $20 is the highest you would have to promise to get a completed questionnaire. For Guerrillas conducting their first mail study, it is prudent to conduct a number of pilot mailings using several incentive variations. Mail 100 questionnaires to one sample enclosing $1 and $5 upon return. Try 100 with $2 enclosed and $5 upon return. Or if your questionnaire is 12 sides or more, try $2 enclosed with $10 upon return. Since it is impossible to know the target that you might be trying to reach or the length of your questionnaire, it's difficult for me to suggest the exact incentives that will work best. Testing various incentives first is always wise and will provide you with the information you need when conducting future mail studies.

- *Internet studies.* When conducting internet studies, it is only necessary to pay incentives when the questionnaire is completed. Usually the same completion incentives used for mail questionnaires will work for internet questionnaires. Nevertheless, it is wise to find a company that specializes in conducting internet studies to advise you on incentives. What is nice about the internet is that you can test different incentives almost daily in order to optimize the response.

14

How to conduct surveys

It is best to have read the previous chapter on sampling before reading this chapter. If you are here and have skipped Chapter 13, go back and read it now.

There are five major approaches for collecting data for quantitative studies. They are:

1. telephone;
2. mail;
3. in-person interviews;
4. the internet;
5. panels.

Additionally, these five approaches can be used in tandem. Sometimes respondents are first contacted by phone, questioned, and asked to complete a follow-up mail or internet questionnaire. The same is true for respondents first questioned by the other approaches.

The point is that, once a person has agreed to be interviewed using one technique, a relatively high percentage will be willing to be interviewed on the same topic using another approach. *Determining the best single or dual approach for collecting the needed information is what's ultimately important.*

TELEPHONE INTERVIEWING

Telephone interviewing is probably the most popular approach for collecting data. There are large numbers of telephone interviewing services that specialize in telephone interviewing for market research purposes. They hire and train interviewers and administer questionnaires that are written by professional researchers. They, themselves, don't employ professional market research people. Their sole purpose is to complete the desired number of interviews among a designated population group – as instructed by their professional research clients.

There are many market research companies that also hire and train telephone interviewers as well as provide professional services. These tend to be particularly the large, full-service research suppliers that can design your survey, write your questionnaire, conduct the interviews, and process and analyze your results.

Simply go to Google using the key words "telephone interviewing services" and add your country to your search instruction. You can also find either full-service suppliers or telephone interviewing suppliers throughout the world by going to www.quirks.com or www.bluebook.org.

Collecting data over the phone has the following advantages:

- Along with panels, the telephone is considered the best approach for generating a projectable sample of respondents.
- It is a very efficient approach for interviewing large numbers of respondents.
- It allows the collection of a great deal of information quickly.
- It is economical, especially when the respondents to be interviewed are a large percentage of the population.
- It is relatively fast to complete a study.

It has the following disadvantages:

- Generally, the longest you can keep a person on the phone is 20 minutes. Interviews that are longer might require an incentive to the respondent to complete the interview.
- It can become expensive for small population groups, when less than 10 percent of the population might qualify as potential respondents.
- Telemarketing services attempting to sell are often lumped together with legitimate market research services causing more and more people to hang up.
- It isn't good for certain kinds of questioning procedures in which a respondent is required to read concepts or ideas or see lists or pictures in order to give meaningful responses.

Telephone interviewing costs

Table 14.1 gives an example of costs for conducting telephone interviews. It illustrates the cost per interview (CPI) for a 5-, 10-, 15-, or 20-minute interview as well as for various incidence rates. The incidence rate refers to the percentage of consumers who are expected to qualify as the respondents you wish to interview. If 100 percent of people in your survey qualify to be interviewed (which is rarely the case), and you are going to question them for only 5 minutes, you would pay $7.50 for each completed interview or $750 for 100 interviews, $7,500 for 1,000 interviews, etc.

If only one in 10 people qualify to be interviewed – a 10 percent incidence – and you want to interview them for 20 minutes, you would pay $72.50 for each completed interview.

These figures are only your cost for collecting your data. They don't include what you would pay a full-service supplier for writing your questionnaire, tabulating your data, or analyzing your results. Of course, if you undertook all the activities of a full-service supplier yourself, your only expense would be the telephone service.

Table 14.1 Example of per-interview costs when estimating a telephone interview

Incidence %	5 minutes $	10 minutes $	15 minutes $	20 minutes $
100	7.50	12.50	18.50	24.50
90	8.00	13.00	19.00	25.00
85	8.50	13.50	19.50	25.50
80	8.75	13.75	19.75	25.75
75	9.25	14.25	20.25	26.25
70	9.75	14.75	20.75	26.75
65	10.25	15.25	21.25	27.25
60	11.00	16.00	22.00	28.00
50	12.75	17.75	23.75	29.75
40	15.50	20.50	26.50	32.50
30	19.75	24.75	30.75	36.75
25	23.50	28.50	34.50	40.50
20	28.75	33.75	39.75	45.75
10	55.50	60.50	66.50	72.50

Source: APC Research, Chicago

Table 14.1 illustrates how one telephone interviewing service sets its prices. Notice the lower the incidence rate and the longer the interview, the more costly it is to complete each interview. Because this is only an example, interviewing cost will certainly vary from service to service.

MAIL SURVEYS

Mail surveys are the most economical way to collect data. As such, they are particularly efficient for collecting large quantities of information among large samples of people. As a rule of thumb, mail data collection is about half the cost of telephone data collection.

Most important when using a mail survey is to ensure that you are generating a projectable sample of respondents.

Let's say you send out a four-page questionnaire on the topic of life insurance to 2,000 men at random. Even if you included a postage-paid return envelope, you would be lucky if 5 percent responded. Although you would have 100 completed questionnaires, the low response rate would invalidate the data. You'd be left wondering whether the opinions of the 1,900 who didn't respond are the same as those of the 100 who did.

Some marketers won't use mail survey data unless at least 50 percent respond. In my experience, a 35 percent response rate will generate valid data: that is, if the study were to be conducted a second time with a 35 percent response rate, results would be the same as in the first study.

There are a number of ways to stimulate higher response rates. They are:

1. Always use money. Include a $1 bill, or better yet a $2 bill, when you mail the questionnaire. With a four-page questionnaire, offer an additional $10 when the completed questionnaire is returned. For a longer questionnaire, offer more (e.g., $20 for eight pages).
2. Along with the money, identify yourself as the sponsor. People are far more likely to respond if they know who is sponsoring the study.
3. Do step 1 or steps 1 and 2 after you have sent out a letter announcing the study. This alerts people to the fact that the questionnaire is on the way and provides additional legitimacy.
4. Do all the above steps and provide a lottery bonus. Offer an additional $200 if the respondent's name is pulled out from the names of a pool of people who respond.
5. Always provide a date for return. From the approximate date of receipt of the questionnaire, give no more than three weeks to respond.

6. Even the best planning might not generate a good response. Therefore consider pilot-testing your questionnaire. Sending out 200 question-naires is enough to determine if you are hitting your response goals. If not, consider increasing the incentive, shortening the questionnaire, or doing both.

There are certainly other factors that influence response rates. They include the nature of the topic, the ease with which the questionnaire can be completed, and the time of year it is sent (between Thanksgiving and Christmas is always a terrible time for mail questionnaires). Nevertheless, the incentive that you offer and the length of your questionnaire are always the most important.

Mail questionnaires have *advantages* when:

- You have a great deal of information to collect.
- You have pictures, illustrations, concepts, or ideas and it is necessary for respondents to see or read material in order to provide thoughtful responses.
- You know how to design a questionnaire that is easy to read and simple to complete.
- You can easily access the names and addresses of people whose opinions are important.
- You can afford the extra four to six weeks that it takes to conduct a mail study as opposed to a phone study.

Mail questionnaires are at a distinct *disadvantage* when:

- You have open-ended questions. People will easily check boxes, but if you ask them to write in why they feel a certain way don't expect much more than superficial responses.
- You want to control the manner in which questions are seen. If seeing one part of the questionnaire is important before seeing other parts, using a mail questionnaire poses a problem. Respondents will often read the entire questionnaire to see all the questions being asked before filling it out.
- You have a complex questionnaire. Respondents can follow very simple instructions for skipping from one question to another or one section of the questionnaire to another section. But if it requires complex skip patterns, respondents can become frustrated and give up the questionnaire altogether.

IN-PERSON INTERVIEWING

Years ago, interviewers would go door to door to administer question-naires. They would follow a complex series of instructions to determine what neighborhood to go to, what street to start on, and the exact house to go to, all in an effort to generate a random projectable sample of respon-dents. Today, in-person door-to-door interviewing is both unsafe and economically impractical.

In survey research, personal interviews are most often conducted when it is necessary to show respondents exhibits, have them taste food products, or give them products to take home and use. This doesn't mean that in-person interviewing is an unpopular approach for collecting data – quite the contrary.

In every major city in the world there are market research field services located in shopping center malls. Go to www.bluebook.org or www.quirks.com for a free listing of mall facilities. These central location mall facilities are the primary source for conducting in-person interviews.

You may have encountered interviewers in the shopping centers you use. They first ask a series of questions to determine if the person stopped qual-ifies to be interviewed. If so, that person may be interviewed on the spot or asked to accompany the interviewer to a nearby research location

Sometimes, respondents are pre-recruited by phone and paid $25, $50, or more and given an appointment time to be interviewed at the mall facility. And, on rare occasions, an interviewer might go to the respondent's home to conduct the interview. Obviously, this would be a more expensive approach to personal interviewing, but, depending on the study and the type of respondent that is needed, it may be the best approach.

Central location mall intercept interviewing is optimal when it is necessary for respondents to be presented with something before they are asked to respond. This could be:

- ads, concepts, storyboards, new product idea boards, promotion materials, catalogs;
- packages, packaging graphics, packing sizes;
- products to observe and comment upon;
- products to taste before commenting;
- products to take home and use;
- product displays.

Additionally, there could be other types of research studies that require complex interviewing approaches making it necessary for the interviewer to be physically present to ensure that the interview is undertaken properly.

Mall intercept interviewing has a number of problems associated with it. They include:

- *Not generating a nationally projectable random sample.* Say you collect 150 mall interviews in one city and 150 in another. Even though you have collected 300 interviews, which is enough for a good sample, you really are only representing the opinions of shoppers in those cities who shop at those malls. Your findings might not represent the attitudes of people who shop at other malls in those cities much less those of people who live and shop in other cities.
- *Finding low-incidence respondents.* If you are after people who might be difficult to find (e.g., men with size 13 feet or larger, women who wear four-inch heels), it might take you forever to find the right people. This can be very costly.
- *Consistency from one mall location to another.* In any research study, you want to control as much as possible the manner in which interviewers administer the questionnaire. You don't want them going at it one way in one location and another way in another location. This is always a challenge when conducting mall intercept studies in a number of markets.

THE INTERNET

The internet is becoming more popular for collecting market research data. Its chief advantages include being potentially very fast and very inexpensive. The chief disadvantage, *and it is a big one*, is the reliability and projectability of the results.

Think about all the e-mail spam you get and how quickly you delete e-mails that look suspicious or hold very little interest. An invitation to complete a survey is often met with just such a reaction. Because of this, it becomes extremely important to understand how the internet should be used to conduct a survey. Response rates to questionnaires that are e-mailed randomly are most problematic, sometimes generating less than a 5 percent response rate.

Response is also influenced by the length and complexity of the questionnaire, whether a legitimate company is sponsoring the study, and the nature of the topic.

Unless you are very careful, conducting a study over the internet can be worse than not conducting one at all.

As with any quantitative market research study, it is important that results be projectable. And you need to be careful to ensure that the people providing you with answers are the people whose opinions you want, and not just people who spend hours clicking on banner ads that invite them to complete a questionnaire or are prone to reading and responding to every e-mail that arrives.

There are many market research companies that are experienced when it comes to conducting research over the internet. Check on www.bluebook.org or www.quirks.com for a listing of some. You can even search Google, Yahoo, or Ask Jeeves using the key words "internet surveys" to learn everything you'd ever want to know about internet research.

The internet should not be ruled out as a great way of conducting research, but it's not something you should try without first consulting with several research suppliers that have experience with this mode of data collection.

Assuming you are intrigued and curious about the internet, and have the time, check out three or four suppliers or consultants with internet experience. Make sure you do your due diligence by determining:

- Whether they have software readily available for conducting online surveys. If not, they are likely to be internet research novices. If you are technically inclined and ambitious, click on www.camsp.com/index.php for information on creating internet questionnaires.
- The response rate that they have achieved when using the internet and an explanation of what they did to achieve higher rates.
- How they recommend that you identify the types of respondents you want for your survey.
- How they would recommend you could achieve a representative and projectable sample of respondents.

Even though the internet is considered to be faster and less expensive than using the telephone, it would be prudent to estimate your study both ways. Sometimes the telephone is less cumbersome and a more reliable means of conducting your survey. And if the cost is higher, it might be only marginally so.

PANELS

In the early 1950s consumer mail panels were formed for the purpose of conducting market research studies. The early panels consisted of several hundred thousand people. Panel members were solicited by mail, asked if they would like to participate in market research surveys from time to time, and promised products or other incentives to participate. The early panels were very successful.

Today, panels are extremely sophisticated and a great way to collect information, often quite inexpensively. Panels consist of hundreds of thousands of members in many different countries who can be used to survey almost any consumer product and most business-to-business products or services. Panel members can be interviewed using telephone, mail, or the internet.

Because members are pre-screened for their willingness to fill out surveys, response rates are extremely high. This allows panel studies to be easily designed to be representative and projectable.

What is unusual about panels is that they have large databases of information about their members. All member demographics are on file, as are many other characteristics that relate to areas such as automobiles, financial products, health care, information technology, and package goods usage. That allows easy access to specific members whose opinions are important and to people who might be difficult to locate when conducting a random survey. Hard-to-find respondents can be people with certain diseases or ailments, those who drive a particular make of car, men over 65 who like deep-sea fishing, or others who undertake unique activities.

Additionally, some panels collect syndicated data that can be purchased by anyone wishing to use the data. Purchasing syndicated data can be far less expensive than conducting a custom study and much faster. It is generally prudent to check with the panels to determine whether information that they routinely capture would serve your needs.

When all is said and done, though, panels are not a panacea. They are not efficient for collecting information from customers who might be on an in-house database. And while costs for some types of studies can be very reasonable, for others they can be quite costly.

There are a relatively small number of mail panels. Here are some that cover the United States as well as operating in various countries throughout the world:

- www.synovate.com;
- www.tns-global.com;
- www.ipsos-insight.com;
- www.surveypro.com.

In-person, mail, internet, and panel interview costs

There are so many factors affecting costs when conducting in-person, mail, internet, and panel studies that it is difficult to provide rule-of-thumb figures that can be compared to the telephone costs that were previously illustrated. Nevertheless, I have found the following to be generally true:

- Costs for mail surveys are highly dependent on the incentives that must be used to generate respondent cooperation. Nevertheless, mail studies can run at almost 50 percent less cost than telephone studies.
- Costs for conducting personal interviews via random mall intercepts are approximately the same to 15 percent higher than telephone costs.
- Costs for conducting internet interviews are also highly dependent on the incentives that must be paid to generate respondent cooperation. You can usually figure, though, that you will save 25 percent to 50 percent over telephone interviewing costs.

Panel costs tend to be unpredictable. Sometimes they are extremely low and other times very expensive.

Since panels ensure the privacy of their members and will not release their names, you must use their in-house interviewing staff when conducting telephone interviews. Costs here tend to be 15 percent to 25 percent higher than using a regular telephone field service.

Costs for panel mail studies can be quite reasonable and run almost 50 percent lower than using a regular telephone field service. Panel interviewing using their internet panel is about 20 percent lower than using the panel for telephone questioning.

15

Organizing data

Surveys require that questions be tabulated and be formatted so that answers can be effectively analyzed. The most common format for accomplishing this is through a cross-tabulation program (referred to as "crosstabs").

The cost of tabulating survey data has reached an all-time low, especially when conducting telephone studies. In the past, it was necessary for keypunch operators to hand-punch the answer to each and every question asked on each and every questionnaire. Although the labor cost for this process was relatively low, it was nevertheless a cost that had to be incurred.

Today, there are still studies that require questionnaires to be manually keypunched. In-person, mall intercept, and mail questionnaires are the most common examples. Even here, some upfront planning with your supplier will allow your questionnaires to be set up for optical scanning – which can save you both time and money. But now, most telephone field services program questionnaires on computer-assisted telephone interviewing (CATI) systems, which not only make interviewing faster and easier but also eliminate the need for any type of data entry whatsoever.

Costs for cross-tabs are dependent on the number of questionnaires that you are tabulating as well as the number of questions asked. Long questionnaires with large samples may cost $2,500 to $3,000 or more to tabulate, especially if key entry or open-ended coding of questions is necessary. Often, your study will be smaller and your tab bill much more economical. And, again, by eliminating manual keypunch entry, you can save upwards of 50 percent on your tab bill.

CROSS-TAB PLAN

In order to have data tabulated to meet your needs, you should create a cross-tab plan. Creating the tab plan will help you to determine how you want to "cut your data," that is, how you want to see data arrayed for the questions that you've asked. In other words, a tab plan shows the way the data will be organized and presented, and serves as a document for your tabulation company so it can prepare the data the way you want.

In determining the tab plan, you will make assumptions as to the segments of the data that might be important to analyze. Obviously, you will tabulate the data in total. If your sample size is 600, you will look at how all 600 respondents answered all the questions. But it is beyond the total that your most important analysis is likely to exist.

Popcorn study

Let's say that you have conducted an attitude study among 600 respondents on the topic of popcorn. You have the following overall objective: "To understand the important factors when choosing to purchase one brand of popcorn over another. To determine the extent to which the brands on the market are perceived to deliver on the factors that are important."

Specific objectives are:

- How do various segments of the market differ on attitudes that are important – heavy versus light popcorn users, large versus small families, etc.?
- Do users of the various brands have different attitudes toward factors that are important?
- Are there differences in attitudes of consumers who use microwave popcorn most often versus consumers who pop from scratch?
- What are the attitudes toward potential new flavors of popcorn? Will new flavors cause greater consumption of popcorn?

Tab plan implication

Your tab plan should reflect the study objectives. Look at the objective and think about the tab plan implication.

Since the goal is to determine brand perceptions, you will want to view how the major brands on the market are perceived. This would suggest organizing or tabulating the data by brand. Assume that the major brands you are most interested in are:

- Orville Redenbacher;
- Paul Newman;
- Pop Secret.

Also, given the specific objective ("How do various segments of the market differ on attitudes that are important – heavy versus light popcorn users, large versus small families, etc.?"), the tab plan implication might be first to make an assumption as to a definition of heavy versus light popcorn users. In your questionnaire, you will certainly have asked a question regarding frequency of using popcorn at home.

In developing a tab plan, it is often necessary to have your tab supplier provide you with total counts (which should be free of charge) on certain questions before you make a final decision about the plan. In this case, that is what you should do.

Table 15.1 shows the questions on popcorn consumption that you might have asked and the typical answers you might have received.

A heavy versus light definition could be determined by simply splitting the sample above and below the mean. Here the mean is about once a week. So you could decide to organize the data into two groups with those using more than once a week becoming heavy users, and those using less than once a week becoming light users.

From Table 15.1, the split would generate 228 heavy users (adding together the 3 percent, 5 percent, 10 percent, and 20 percent and multiplying by the 600 respondents in the study) and 372 light users (adding together all the rest).

Table 15.1   Popcorn consumption example

"How often do you pop and eat popcorn at home?"	%
Every day	3
Four to six times per week	5
One to three times per week	10
About once per week	20
Once every two weeks	25
Once every three to four weeks	20
Once a month	10
Less often than once per month	7
	Mean = once every 6.60 days

Another way is just to make a judgment based on the frequency of responses. You could decide to combine some groups. You could take the three times a week and more respondents (18 percent total), giving you 108 respondents, which is a good base of respondents to analyze. You could combine the once a week and once every two weeks (45 percent) to generate 270 respondents. The remaining 37 percent would give you 222 respondents.

This approach would give you three user definitions:

- Heavy users = 108.
- Regular users = 270.
- Light users = 222.

If you want to set size of family, income, or other breaks for example, you could go through the same process.

These are important judgments that you must make in determining how you wish to organize and view your data. In these instances, there is rarely a right and wrong approach. Decisions are usually based on common sense and the actions you might take if your analysis shows major differences between groups.

Another specific objective is to determine if there are differences in attitudes of consumers who use microwave popcorn most often as opposed to consumers who pop from scratch. Here the tab plan implication is that you should organize the data by microwave users versus pop-from-scratch users.

But the question becomes how to do this. Since many families do both, perhaps you ask several questions in your questionnaire regarding usage. You might have asked:

What do you pop at home most often – microwave popcorn or pop-from-scratch popcorn?

You could have asked:

How often do you pop and eat microwave popcorn at home?
- Every day
- Four to six times per week
- One to three times per week
- About once per week
- Once every two weeks
- Once every three to four weeks
- Once a month
- Less often than once per month

How often do you pop and eat pop-from-scratch popcorn at home?
- Every day
- Four to six times per week
- One to three times per week
- About once per week
- Once every two weeks
- Once every three to four weeks
- Once a month
- Less often than once per month

If you used this more complex series of questions in determining microwave versus pop-from-scratch usage, the data could be organized more precisely and the analysis would be more insightful.

BANNER POINT AND STUB

When you complete your tab plan, your tab supplier will prepare the data to your specifications. The final result will be a printout of all the questions in your questionnaire organized and tabulated by all the ways you wish to view the data. In relation to this, you should be aware of the terms "banner points" and "stub."

"Banner points" refer to the number of breakouts that a printout will accommodate. Typically you can choose about 20 breakouts, banner points, or data cuts in your tabulated report. "Stub" refers to the questions that were asked.

Look at a typical printout, as shown in Table 15.2. Down the left side of the printout page is the stub or the question that was asked. Across the top of the page is the banner or the way the data are organized.

When you complete your tab plan, you may have specified up to 20 banner points that you want on your printout. If you wish to organize the data beyond 20 banner points, you'll simply request that a second banner be developed. Once you have set up your first banner, the cost of a second banner is quite nominal.

You will also have indicated how you want your stub to appear. In the printout example in Table 15.2, notice the question stub and you will see what are referred to as "nets." A net refers to the sum or total of two or more answers to a given question. In this example, four responses are given.

The net here is simply the sum of the 3s and 2s and the 1s and 0s. By showing the net score in the stub, it saves time in analyzing the data, since a quick glance indicates the percentage of respondents having generally

Table 15.2 Typical tabulation printout of survey data

XYZ retail copy, print and delivery study

Q. amount would use XYZ if they did the following allow you to check the status of your job online

| | | | Users | | | In home user | | | | | Business user | | | |
| | | | | Business | | Amount spent on copying | | | Household size | | Amount spent on copying | | | |
	TOTAL (A)	In home (B)	1-5 (C)	6-19 (D)	Total (E)	$50 to $99 (F)	$100 to $299 (G)	$300+ (H)	2 or Less (I)	3+ (J)	$299 or Less (K)	$300 to $999 (L)	$1000 to $2999 (M)	$3000+ (N)
TOTAL	475	175	150	150	300	84	47	40	77	82	76	84	43	42
Net: Top 2 Box	218 45.9%	68 38.9%	81 54.0% B	69 46.0%	150 50.0% B	30 35.7%	17 36.2%	19 47.5%	23 29.9%	39 47.6% I	45 59.2%	40 47.6%	21 48.8%	19 45.2%
3 – For all my copying and printing jobs	107 22.5%	39 22.3%	43 28.7% D	25 16.7%	68 22.7% B	16 19.0%	11 23.4%	12 30.0%	13 16.9%	24 29.3% i	21 27.6%	18 21.4%	11 25.6%	11 26.2%
2 – For most of my jobs	111 23.4%	29 16.6%	38 25.3% b	44 29.3% B	82 27.3% B	14 16.7%	6 12.8%	7 17.5%	10 13.0%	15 18.3%	24 31.6%	22 26.2%	19 23.3%	8 19.0%
1 – For just an occasional job	143 30.1%	55 31.4%	39 26.0%	49 32.7%	88 29.3%	27 32.1%	18 38.3%	10 25.0%	25 32.5%	27 32.9%	20 26.3%	30 35.7%	14 32.6%	11 26.2%
0 – For none of my copying and printing jobs	90 18.9%	32 18.3%	27 18.0%	31 20.7%	58 19.3%	19 22.6% G	3 6.4%	8 20.0% g	18 23.4% J	9 11.0%	10 13.2%	14 16.7%	8 18.6%	11 26.2% k
Net: Bottom 2 Box	233 49.1%	87 49.7%	66 44.0%	80 53.3%	146 48.7%	46 54.8%	21 44.7%	18 45.0%	43 55.8%	36 43.9%	30 39.5%	44 52.4%	22 51.2%	22 52.4%
Don't know	24 5.1%	20 11.4% CDE	3 2.0%	1 0.7%	4 1.3%	8 9.5%	9 19.1%	3 7.5%	11 14.3%	7 8.5%	1 1.3%	0 –	0 –	1 2.4%
Mean	1.52	1.48	1.66	1.42	1.54	1.36	1.66	1.62	1.27	1.72	1.75	1.52	1.56	1.46
Std Devn	1.06	1.08	1.09	1.00	1.05	1.08	0.99	1.16	1.07	1.05	1.01	1.01	1.08	1.16

NOTE: Significance Testing done at the following levels: Upper case letters = 95 percent, lower case letters = 90 percent
Groups/pairs tested: B/C/D/E, F/G/H I/J, K/L/M/N

positive attitudes on the question as opposed to those having generally neutral or negative attitudes. The analyst doesn't have to add the two together.

TAB PLAN EXAMPLE

Below is an example of how to write out a tab plan thus indicating how you want the cross-tabs arrayed. It calls for 19 banner points and features the number of the question in the questionnaire from which each banner point is derived. It also highlights the base number of respondents for some of the banner points. The question number and the base number of respondents are for the tab supplier's benefit, making it easier to set up the correct banner specifications.

Further, it provides instructions for desired significance tests. Note that statistical tests will be provided at the 95 percent and 90 percent confidence levels.

1. Total (Base = 325).
2. 1 to 19 company employees (Q.14).
3. 20 to 49 company employees (Q.14).
4. 50 to 99 company employees (Q.14).
5. 100 or more company employees (Q.14).
6. Company revenue less than $500,000 (Q.16).
7. Company revenue $500,000 to $1,000,000 (Q.16).
8. Company revenue $1 million to $10 million (Q.16).
9. Company revenue $10 million plus (Q.16).
10. Most often use source for printing and copying services (Q.11a Base = 68).
11. Use "other" sources most often for printing and copying (Q.11a Base = 222).
12. Have used Alpha for printing and copying in the past (Q.12a Base = 88).
13. Have not used Alpha for printing in past (Q.12a Base = 169).
14. Company receives special printing and copying discounts from Alpha (Q.13c).
15. Company does not receive special printing discounts from Alpha (Q.13c).
16. Company industry – professional (includes accounting, banking, education, health care, law services, real estate).
17. Company industry – industrial (includes construction, manufacturing, transportation).
18. Receive special bonus promotions from Alpha (Q.13d).

19. Receive special bonus promotions from other companies (Q.13d all other companies).

T-tests of significance at 95% and 90%; compare columns 2 through 5, 6 through 9, 10 vs. 11, 12 vs. 13, 14 vs. 15, 16 vs. 17, 18 vs. 19.

While creating a tab plan for yourself is helpful in thinking through how you want to analyze the data, it is not essential. Any market research tabulation supplier that you wish to use will, for little if any cost, help you determine how to set up cross-tabs and create your tab plan.

16

Statistical techniques

Because I am not a statistician, nor do I have any interest in becoming one, I rely on several people who do nothing but crank out special statistical procedures for market researchers. Nevertheless, I have a working knowledge of various techniques that are available and a general understanding of when it is appropriate to use them. You should as well – and they are set out in the following sections.

SIGNIFICANCE TESTS

The majority of research studies do not require use of sophisticated statistical techniques in order to analyze the data. In fact, simply tabulating the data and looking at the responses is often enough to give you clear answers. Nevertheless, data in surveys should always be subjected to tests of significance.

A significance test, or what is referred to as a "t-test," tells you whether there is a difference between two sets of data. This is a simple, inexpensive program that you should make sure is applied to your study tabulations.

Look at Table 16.1. If you asked the question of 200 beer drinkers whether they would try a new lemon-flavored beer, the error range would be +/–7 percent. With 60 percent saying yes and 40 percent saying no, a t-test would say that we can be 95 percent confident in concluding that more beer drinkers like the idea than don't like it.

Table 16.1   Attitude toward lemon-flavored beer – no statistical difference

	Total	Heavy beer drinkers	Light beer drinkers
Number of interviews:	200	100	100
Question: "Would you try a new beer if it contained a touch of lemon in the flavor?"			
Yes	60%	55%	65%
No	40%	45%	35%

But with a sample size of 100 heavy beer drinkers and 100 light beer drinkers, the error range around this smaller sample size would be +/–10 percent. Therefore, the t-test would indicate that you can be 95 percent confident that there is no difference between the answers given by heavy beer drinkers and those given by light beer drinkers. That is, heavy and light beer drinkers like the idea of a lemon-flavored beer to the same degree, even though the 55 percent as against 65 percent figures alone might lead you to conclude otherwise.

A reminder about 95 percent confidence levels: Confidence levels refer to the answers you are likely to get if you repeat a research study exactly the same way again and again and again. In this case, it would indicate that there is a 95 percent chance that the above numbers would not vary more than the statistical error range. Stated another way, there is only a 5 percent chance that you would reach a different conclusion as to the appeal of a lemon-flavored beer if the study were repeated.

In market research studies, the rule of thumb is to use a 95 percent confidence level when conducting tests of significance and making decisions. Nevertheless, it is sometimes reasonable to make conclusions and decisions using 90 percent or even 85 percent levels of confidence. Please be aware that, for no additional cost, you can order tabulations that will test your data at 95 percent, 90 percent, or 85 percent confidence levels.

Table 16.2 shows another example of significance testing. In this case, there is a 20 percentage point difference between the answers given by heavy as opposed to light beer drinkers. With the same error range of +/–10 percent, the t-test would tell you that you can be 95 percent confident that the difference is statistically significant. You could then conclude that light beer drinkers are, in fact, more likely to try a new lemon-flavored beer than are heavy beer drinkers and would be a better target for the new product than would heavy beer drinkers.

Table 16.3 gives another example that illustrates what happens when you increase the sample size. It shows exactly the same answers as illustrated in

Table 16.2 Attitude toward lemon-flavored beer – statistical difference

	Total	Heavy beer drinkers	Light beer drinkers
Number of interviews:	200	100	100
Question: "Would you try a new beer if it contained a touch of lemon in the flavor?"			
Yes	60%	50%	70%
No	40%	50%	30%

Table 16.3 Attitude toward lemon-flavored beer – increased sample size

	Total	Heavy beer drinkers	Light beer drinkers
Number of interviews:	300	150	150
Question: "Would you try a new beer if it contained a touch of lemon in the flavor?"			
Yes	60%	55%	65%
No	40%	45%	35%

Table 16.1, only this time 300 total interviews were conducted instead of 200, with 150 each among heavy and light beer drinkers instead of 100. Even with the larger samples of 150, the error range would be +/–8 percent and the t-test would show that there is no statistical difference. Therefore, with these results and the brilliance of hindsight you would have learned the same thing with a less costly research study and the 200 sample size.

Here, in other words, even with sample sizes of 150 per target the difference between the 55 percent of heavy beer drinkers and 65 percent of light beer drinkers saying that they would try the new beer is not great enough to produce a statistically significant difference at the 95 percent confidence level.

A word about larger sample sizes

As discussed earlier, cost is always a factor in determining how many respondents you can afford to interview. Nevertheless, there is a point at which choosing to go with a sample size that is too small is as wasteful as going overboard with a sample size that is too large. In the case of the 55/65 percent split, 100 respondents per target proved too small to allow a significant difference. When the difference was 50 percent as against 70 percent, the sample size showed significance.

Again, it is inexpensive and good practice to have your survey data subjected to t-testing. It is the only way to know if one set of answers is different from the next.

Now, if you only knew the results before you did your studies, you would then be able to know the minimum sample size you would need for statistically valid results and could spend as little as possible getting actionable results.

REGRESSION ANALYSIS

Regression analysis seeks to determine the factors that are important in causing action. Let's say you did a survey, asked "How likely are you to buy from Wal-Mart in the next seven days?" and got the answers indicated in Table 16.4.

In the same study you also asked respondents to rate Wal-Mart against four statements and got the answers given in Table 16.5.

Here are two different sets of data. One indicates the intent to shop at Wal-Mart and the other indicates the rating of Wal-Mart on four statements. It would be reasonable to assume that Wal-Mart wants to motivate as many people as possible to shop at a Wal-Mart store in the next seven days. By doing a regression analysis it is possible to determine which of the four statements has the greatest correlation with intention to shop. In other words, which statement most strongly relates to the likelihood of shopping at Wal-Mart in the next seven days?

For example, assume that "Gives me one-stop shopping" has the strongest correlation with intention to shop. This would suggest a totally

Table 16.4 Example of likelihood-to-purchase question

"How likely are you to buy from Wal-Mart in the next seven days?"	
Will definitely buy	30%
Will probably buy	20%
Might or might not buy	15%
Will probably not buy	20%
Will definitely not buy	15%

Table 16.5 Example of typical agree/disagree rating question

"Please rate the extent to which you agree or disagree with the following statements that describe Wal-Mart."

Walmart:	Agree strongly %	Agree somewhat %	Disagree strongly %	Disagree somewhat %
Is convenient to my home	40	30	15	15
Has the lowest prices	35	50	10	5
Gives me one-stop shopping	30	30	30	10
Has great customer service	20	20	20	40

different advertising and promotion approach from that suggested by "Has the lowest prices."

By the same token, assume that there is a strong correlation with the statement "Has great customer service." But only 20 percent agree strongly that Wal-Mart has great customer service. This suggests that, if Wal-Mart takes action to increase perceptions of customer service, intention to shop will also increase.

This is a very simple explanation to a rather complex statistical procedure. What is important to remember about regression analysis is that it can help explain the actions you should take to achieve the customer behavior you want.

If you are studying how to get heavy and light customers to shop at your store more often, one regression analysis will point out the key areas to focus on for heavy customers, and a second will show the priorities for light customers.

TURF ANALYSIS

TURF stands for "total unduplicated reach and frequency." TURF analysis was originally devised for use in media campaigns and has been expanded to apply elsewhere. This statistical model can be used to answer questions like:

- Where should we place ads to reach the widest possible audience?
- What kind of market share will we gain if we add a new product to the product line we currently sell?
- Will new customers be gained if we add a new flavor, color, scent, or formula to the line of products we currently sell?

- What combination of messages should be communicated in our advertising, promotion, or other selling literature to motivate the greatest number of consumers to take the actions we want?

Table 16.6 shows a practical example of how TURF works. Assume you have 10 messages you could communicate to prospects that would motivate them to visit your shoe store. The messages are shown in the table with the percentage of people who indicated the message is important in causing them to shop.

In just looking at the messages, five are extremely important to 50 percent or more of the prospects. A TURF analysis will determine the number of respondents who will be motivated to visit the store, given various combinations of messages. Table 16.7 illustrates this.

Table 16.6 Rating of factors that motivate purchase

		People indicating message is important %
1.	Lowest price	65
2.	Widest selection	60
3.	Money-back guarantee	55
4.	Knowledgeable salespeople	50
5.	Fast service	50
6.	Well-known brands	45
7.	Discounts for frequent purchasing	35
8.	Open 18 hours a day, seven days a week	30
9.	Convenient parking	25
10.	Play area for children	15

Table 16.7 Reach achieved when combining the top five factors

		Coverage %
1.	Lowest price	45
2.	Fast service	66
3.	Knowledgeable salespeople	70
4.	Money-back guarantee	72
5.	Widest selection	75

It indicates that the lowest price message is important to 45 percent of prospects in motivating them to visit the store. Lowest price and fast service combined will motivate 66 percent. Low price, fast service, and knowledgeable salespeople will motivate 70 percent, and so forth.

A TURF analysis will rank order and put in priority the important messages, new products, new product formulations, line extensions, etc. in the combinations that will reach the most possible customers or prospects.

CLUSTER ANALYSIS

Cluster analysis is a sophisticated data analysis tool. It sorts respondents into groups, or clusters, so that the degree of association is strong between respondents in one cluster and weak between members of different clusters. In other words, it determines the degree to which respondents in each cluster hold the same attitudes or opinions.

Below are three groups of people and the characteristics that cluster together to describe each. Again, the statistical program first puts statements into groupings and then assigns each respondent the group, or cluster, that best reflects their attitudes. Once the statistical program forms the clusters, the research analyst gives each a name that is felt to describe that cluster. The following are examples:

- *Cluster 1 – good-time Joes:*
    - love parties;
    - celebrate whenever possible;
    - enjoy being the center of attention;
    - love to tell stories.
- *Cluster 2 – involved observers:*
    - enjoy movies and plays;
    - would rather listen to stories others tell;
    - enjoy historical novels;
    - take joy in the accomplishments of others.
- *Cluster 3 – wallflowers:*
    - hate crowds;
    - don't go out unless invited;
    - find it hard to make new friends;
    - like to watch soap operas on TV.

Cluster analysis is a technique for better understanding how consumers view themselves, the world around them, or the products or services you sell. By knowing personality types such as the ones described above, marketers can determine the kinds of appeals that are most likely to motivate each cluster grouping.

In this example, once the good-time Joes, involved observers, and wall-flowers clusters are determined, they would become part of the cross-tab banner. This allows determination as to whether differences exist in how clusters answered the other questions in your questionnaire. Having greater insight into the personalities of the respondents and the clusters they belong to gives marketers a unique advantage when creating marketing and advertising programs or when targeting new products or services.

OTHER STATISTICAL TECHNIQUES

For most Guerrillas analyzing research data, it is unnecessary to go beyond basic cross-tabs (as described in Chapter 15) or the few more common statistical techniques previously described. Nevertheless, there are other techniques that are somewhat popular and worth mentioning:

- *Multi-variant analysis* is a tool for combining a wide number of demographic, behavioral, and sometimes attitudinal factors to understand better the groups of consumers that exist and how best to motivate them. If you have a database of customers and a great deal of demographic and behavior data, multi-variant analysis can develop clusters of like consumers based on many factors. A catalog company might, for example, determine how often to mail catalogs or other promotions to various groups in their database based on various combinations of factors. Or a large consumer goods company might determine the best TV programs, magazines, or other media vehicles that work in tandem to reach customers and prospects who have many differing behaviors and demographic patterns.
- *Conjoint analysis* determines the relative importance of one feature over another. For example, when determining which add-on features they want, many new car buyers might say a wide number of features are important and they'd like to have them. But when it comes to the final decision, there is usually a trade-off between the features they might want and the price they'd be willing to pay to get them. Conjoint analysis determines the ultimate combinations of product features and prices that consumers are willing to pay when making purchase decisions. It is a particularly valuable tool when relatively expensive

products (e.g., automobiles, appliances, technology products, home entertainment products, etc.) are being developed or sold. In such cases, it is important for the marketer to understand the features that consumers really want and how much they are willing to pay to get them.

- *Perceptual mapping* is a statistical procedure that compares complex relationships between companies, brands, products, or services and how consumers perceive them. Actual pictorial maps are generated that show how consumers perceive consumer products or companies in terms of their similarities or differences. Perceptual maps are used as a planning tool when conducting sophisticated market segmentation and strategy studies. They also allow marketers to track company or product changes in perceptions from year to year and to evaluate the potential for new products or concepts in a more sophisticated context.

FIGURES DON'T LIE, LIARS FIGURE

You may have heard Brian Williams on NBC reporting on the youth vote in the 2004 U.S. Presidential election. He said something to the effect that all the money spent to get out the youth vote, those 19- to 29-year-old voters, did nothing. He said that 17 percent of the voters who participated in the 2000 election were 19 to 29, which is exactly the same figure as in the 2004 election.

In fact, more 19- to 29-year-olds voted in 2004 than ever before because more people voted in 2004 than in any previous election. The 17 percent share of almost 120 million voters was an astounding 21 million voters. This contrasts with 17 percent of the approximately 95 million voters in 2000, or 16.1 million in the 19- to 29-year-old range – almost 5 million more in 2004 than 2000, a whopping 30 percent increase.

In your market research studies, don't be duped. Remember that numbers only exist in the context of how the questions are asked, how the answers are interpreted, and the statistical reliability that can be attributed to those answers.

17

Telling the story – analyzing survey results

The topic of data analysis is extremely broad. So much of the analytic effort depends on the type and goals of the study. Complex background studies can be analyzed from many points of view and over long periods. They often take a great deal of digging to surface the information that is of ultimate use. Smaller tactical studies may require little more than a glance at the cross-tabs to know the action that is indicated.

Gerry Linda says: "A good analysis tells a story; a consistent, coherent story. Several questions taken together should point to the same conclusions. I don't believe in silver bullets, one statistic that by itself determines what must be done. But I do believe that if you torture all the data long enough it will confess." But just as writing an effective questionnaire is a never-ending learning process, analyzing research data requires a perspective that only experience can bring.

Contained in the data of every study is the story. It may be one that jumps out or one that has to be teased out. There may be consistency in the answers from one question to the next that leads to clear and obvious conclusions. Or the information generated from question to question might take you in circles, leaving you perplexed and confused as to the meaning of the data.

If you are totally new to market research and have yet to work with a set of cross-tabs and what it is telling you, you will be faced with a steep but not insurmountable learning curve. Try following my process.

I always encounter a thick set of cross-tabs with a sense of excitement. To me, the information is a reflection of the time I've spent developing the study objectives, writing the questionnaire, collecting the data, and developing the tab plan. Finally, it's time to see what I've created.

I'm good at devouring data. I can leaf through cross-tabs quickly and spot interesting numbers. Differences between targets pop out quickly. Sometimes questions that I thought would produce interesting information produce little that is valuable. Other times questions that I hadn't anticipated would provide a clear direction happily prove me wrong and form the basis for exciting strategies and precise action plans.

When first analyzing data, I sit quietly with cross-tabs and read the tables. I look at each question and how all the respondents answered. I scan across every table to see if the t-tests identify certain targets answering the question differently.

With a pencil I circle interesting, surprising, or puzzling numbers. Often, it doesn't take long before I have a sense of the data, and a clear story starts to emerge. Other times, the data are bland and uninspiring. The story is wishy-washy and the direction vague. I know it will be a struggle before I tease out the story.

Most times I let the story emerge slowly, over several days, and so should you. Take that first hour or two with the cross-tabs and sit quietly with the data. Familiarize yourself with the answers. Keep in mind that out of confusion will come clarity, and with patience, persistence, determination, and curiosity you will uncover the story told by the data – one that holds together and provides direction that you can be confident in following.

THE ZEN OF DATA

In and of themselves, data have very little meaning. If you describe a new product that you feel has potential in a survey, and 25 percent of the respondents indicate that they would buy it, would you think that's good or bad? If 50 percent of your customers rated your customer service as excellent, would you be happy or unhappy?

The question that you must constantly be asking yourself when analyzing data is: compared to what?

If you had previous research indicating that when you achieve a 25 percent intention-to-buy rating on a survey it will translate into a successful product, then 25 percent is good. If your 50 percent customer service rating compared to a 75 percent rating for your major competitor then you should be unhappy.

You can analyze survey results from many different perspectives. These include:

1. using a control;
2. making comparisons to previous research;
3. making comparisons to industry norms;
4. making comparisons to actual purchase behavior;
5. comparing one target to another;
6. comparing alternatives to each other.

Let's take a look at each.

Using a control

A control can be just about any comparison you can make. In choosing a control, though, there should be the assumption that, in bettering the control, you will have a winner. For example, it could be:

- Your ratings on a new product or new service compared to the ratings on the same product or service that a competitor might have already introduced. This might be the actual product you've developed compared to a competitive product already on the market. It could also be a simple concept statement that describes the benefits of your product compared to the benefits of an existing product.
- Your ratings compared to the ratings for the market leader and/or other competition. Comparisons can be made across any dimension including products or services sold, company image, attitudes, perceptions, or previous experiences.
- Your ratings compared to rating goals that you have set for yourself and are intent on achieving.

When you are using a control as comparison, the goal is at least to meet, and preferably exceed, the scores achieved by your control. If you are developing a new peanut butter, you will presumably want a product that tastes at least as good as a leading control brand. If you test your peanut butter product against the control, and it doesn't meet or exceed acceptance ratings achieved by it, you should probably reformulate your product.

If you have an idea for a new fitness center, your competition might be a nationwide fitness club or a local gym. You could write a one- or two-paragraph "concept" statement that describes the benefits of joining your fitness center and a similar statement for either the nationwide fitness club or the local gym or both. Here, the control would be both competitors. If more consumers in your target didn't rate interest in joining your fitness center over interest in joining at least one of the two control competitors, you should probably rethink your benefits.

Making comparisons to a successful control is one of the most powerful uses of research and presents one of the easiest techniques for analyzing data.

If your objective is to be at least on a par with a successful competitor, the data will quickly reveal whether you should move forward. If your objective is to be twice as good as your competitor, the data will tell you if you are there or if you have more work to do.

Making comparisons to previous research

Another potent control is comparing the results from previous research studies. If you are conducting an image and attitude study, an awareness study, or a customer satisfaction study, you would start with a benchmark study that determines currently existing levels. Follow-up studies conducted at regular intervals are then compared to the benchmark control and progress judged.

Also, previous research levels achieved when introducing new advertising or marketing approaches or new products or services should serve you well, assuming you know how those programs and products performed in the marketplace. If you know that scores achieved in surveys indicate actual market success or failure, you have achieved very powerful control measurements.

Companies that conduct a great deal of research have a strong advantage when considering go/no-go decisions. The scores achieved on previous research can be used as reliable predictors of success. It would be questionable, for example, for HP to introduce a new generation of computer printers unless the scores research testers gave the new printers were better than scores that HP received among testers before it introduced the current generation.

Making comparisons to industry norms

Many market research companies make normative data available to their clients. Research companies that specialize in testing advertising are particularly good in this regard. If you've developed advertising for a new soft drink, for example, you could test your ad or commercial with certain advertising testing companies, and they can tell you how your ad scored versus all the other soft drink ads they've tested.

Other research companies have normative data regarding the scores (also called "hurdle rates") that a new product should achieve before it has a chance of success.

Associations are also a good source of normative data. The Direct Marketing Association (DMA), for example, occasionally conducts studies among consumers buying direct and provides aggregate satisfaction data in regard to the companies from which they purchase. If you are an internet marketer, there are services available that will provide satisfaction scores for people coming to your site as against going to other sites. You can go to any search engine and type in "attitude research" followed by your industry (e.g., "attitude research home remodeling") and you'll find a wealth of information that just might yield extremely valuable normative data.

When you use normative data, you must make sure that you word your questions exactly the same as they are worded in the normative data surveys. That is the only way to effectively compare the data you get from your targets with preexisting norms.

Making comparisons to actual purchase behavior

If you have a database of customers, you have built-in controls for certain types of studies. Perhaps you are trying to determine what changes should be made to motivate certain customer groups to purchase more often. Your control group might be chosen from two customer groups with similar profiles. The difference will be that one group is behaving exactly the way you want, while the other is not. By comparing the attitudes of the two groups, you'll see the areas that need improvement or attention for the lagging group.

Comparing one target to another

In defining the objectives of your study and determining the targets for interviewing, you'll already have made assumptions. Perhaps you'll have determined the control target against which other targets should be compared. If so, your control is obvious and becomes one of your banner points.

In some studies, though, a control might not be obvious. If the purpose of the research is to identify the best targets, you could make some assumptions about a control after you view the initial cross-tab data. This is particularly true when you are conducting background studies aimed at helping you determine strategic direction.

In larger-sample strategic/background studies (600 sample size or more), you'll undoubtedly generate data that allow you to develop various customer or prospect profiles. You could profile customers who you feel are your better customers, your competitors' better customers, or prospects that you think have potential to be converted to your customers. It's quite easy for your tab vendor to combine various characteristics identified in the questionnaire to form groups of respondents who will then make up one or more controls.

Once the characteristics of a control target are determined, you give it a name and make it a banner point in your tabs. Then you are comparing the attitudes of your control group(s) to those of the other groups in your banner. By making such comparisons, the issues that are important for appealing to a wide number of targets will become evident.

Comparing alternatives to each other

There are times when you might find it hard to determine a control. Perhaps your product or service is so unique that comparisons are difficult or meaningless and you are inclined to move ahead without conducting any research.

In cases in which you think control comparisons won't work, consider creating several alternative approaches or benefits for positioning your product or service. Write two or three concepts that stress differing selling approaches and test them against each other. If interest in all the positions that you test appears similarly weak and indicates a lack of enthusiasm, the data may be telling you that the idea is inherently weak. On the other hand, if the data for one position are much stronger than for the other positions, you'll know where your best chance of success lies.

Remember, when looking at data without the benefit of a control, that data that you consider encouraging might really portend a disaster. And data that look discouraging might really indicate a blockbuster success. Without some kind of control, you just can't begin to know.

BEYOND THE FIRST BLUSH

Determining control comparisons is job number one. But now, it's time to look at the data in detail.

Sometimes you can get lucky, and the story is told in your cross-tabs. Additional research analysis or special statistical procedures aren't required to determine the actions that you should take. If the data clearly point the direction and you are in a position to take the appropriate action, you have a successful study and can confidently move forward.

But often you will have to work with the cross-tabs and dig at the data. This means taking data from the cross-tabs and customizing tables. Researchers call it "pulling the data."

The job in pulling data is to array the numbers in the cross-tabs from a different perspective. To do so, researchers usually take a pencil and paper and handwrite new tables. The sections below show examples of how data can be pulled and arrayed.

ANALYZING STRING QUESTIONS

Analyzing string questions is an important challenge when interpreting survey data. Table 17.1 illustrates a typical string question that was asked on a study about catalogs. The question asked was "When buying from clothing catalogs, how important or unimportant is each of the following statements?"

Table 17.1 Example of arraying factors rated as extremely important

	Percentage rating the statement as extremely important:		
	Total	Buy frequently from clothing catalogs	Buy infrequently from clothing catalogs
	%	%	%
Makes it easy to order	58	50	65*
Allows you to return your order for any reason whatsoever	56	41	70*
Has a 100% satisfaction guarantee policy	49	43	55*
Provides free shipping	48	42	53*
Gives you great value for your money	45	30	60*
Has great customer service	34	43*	25
Has the lowest prices	31	11	50*
Has high-quality brands	30	40*	20
Has brands you are aware of	27	39*	15

*indicates a statistically significant difference at the 95% confidence level vs. the opposite column

In looking at Table 17.1, you could make a number of observations. You might look only at the "Total" column and conclude that customer service, lowest prices, high-quality brands, and familiar brands are far less important than the other factors.

In comparing frequent and infrequent buyers, though, you see startling differences. To frequent buyers, great customer service, high-quality brands, and brands that you are aware of are significantly more important than to infrequent buyers. For infrequent buyers, easy to order, easy returns, satisfaction guarantee, free shipping, great value, and lowest prices are of greater significance than to frequent buyers.

Of course, the manner in which you interpret the data is dependent on your marketing goals. If you want to appeal equally to both groups, you would look at the totals and conclude that the best way of doing it is to focus on easy ordering, easy returns, and 100 percent satisfaction.

If, though, you are trying to convince infrequent buyers to buy more frequently you would likely focus more on value, prices, satisfaction, and ease of ordering. To reinforce frequent buyers, you would be likely to remind them about great customer service and the ability to find familiar, high-quality brands.

IMPORTANCE VERSUS AGREEMENT

Once important elements are identified, the question often becomes how well you and/or your competitors are delivering on those elements. Take the catalog statements that are important compared to how catalog company Bob and catalog company Ellie are performing on each element. Table 17.2 shows the elements that are extremely important and whether respondents agree strongly that the Bob and Ellie catalogs are delivering.

The findings from Table 17.2 are that, on allowing returns for any reason and having a 100 percent satisfaction guarantee policy, both catalogs are performing below what the market indicates is extremely important. Neither of the two catalogs is performing at the levels expected by customers and both should focus attention on improving in these areas.

On ease of ordering, having great customer service and great value, both catalogs are performing at or above what the market says is important. Therefore, improvement in these areas is not a priority for either.

Nevertheless, the Bob catalog is at a competitive advantage when it comes to ease of ordering, providing great customer service, having high-quality brands, and having familiar brands. The Ellie catalog would have to improve in these areas if it wants to be more competitive with the Bob catalog.

Table 17.2 Comparison of extremely important factors when rating catalogs

	Rated as extremely important Total %	Agree strongly with the statement when rating the:	
		Bob catalog %	Ellie catalog %
Makes it easy to order	58	70*	60
Allows you to return your order for any reason whatsoever	56	43*	35*
Has a 100% satisfaction guarantee policy	49	40*	35*
Provides free shipping	48	35	53*
Gives you great value for your money	45	45	60*
Has great customer service	34	50*	40
Has the lowest prices	31	25	55*
Has high-quality brands	30	45*	25
Has brands you are aware of	27	40*	20

*indicates a statistical difference at the 95% confidence level to the opposite number (e.g., 70% on "Makes it easy to order" is significantly different from 60%)

Finally, the Ellie catalog is at a competitive advantage when it comes to giving great value for the money, having the lowest prices, and providing free shipping. The Bob catalog would have to improve in these areas if it wants to be more competitive with the Ellie catalog.

GAP ANALYSIS

Another form of analysis is GAP analysis. A GAP score is simply the difference between what consumers say is important and the extent to which they agree it is being delivered. Table 17.3 highlights how GAP scores are derived.

Note that, on "Makes it easy to order," the GAP score is +12. This is simply the "Extremely important" rating subtracted from the Bob catalog rating. The GAP score indicates the extent to which the company is performing better or worse than expected by customers. The +12 score for "Makes it easy to order" indicates that the company is performing better than is actually necessary to meet the expectations of the marketplace. And on the other plus scores, the company is exceeding expectations.

Table 17.3   GAP scores for the Bob catalog

	Rated as extremely important Total %	Agree strongly with the statement when rating the:	
		Bob catalog %	GAP score %
Makes it easy to order	58	70	+12
Allows you to return your order for any reason whatsoever	56	43	−13
Has a 100% satisfaction guarantee policy	49	40	−9
Provides free shipping	48	35	−13
Gives you great value for your money	45	45	0
Has great customer service	34	50	+16
Has the lowest prices	31	25	−6
Has high-quality brands	30	45	+15
Has brands you are aware of	27	40	+13

The −13 score on "Allows you to return your order for any reason whatsoever" and the other minus scores indicate that the company is not meeting the expectations of the marketplace. In the above example, the Bob catalog might consider diverting funds from promoting its brands, where it is over-performing, to creating a more liberal return policy, where it is under-performing.

GAP analysis is a strong tool for understanding where the company should put emphasis. In theory, a company should achieve a 0 score on all factors, which would indicate that it is delivering exactly what the marketplace expects – no more and no less. In reality, though, companies will always over-perform in some areas and under-perform in others.

In fact, by over-performing, companies often arrive at unique positions in the marketplace. Nordstrom has developed a unique position in the market by over-performing when it comes to customer service. Porsche is likely to be perceived as over-performing on automobile performance. And while Wal-Mart probably under-performs on carrying the highest-quality products, it over-performs on providing low prices – which has become its core position and a strong reason for its success.

In all, GAP analysis paints a clear picture of a company's position in the marketplace relative to what might be considered ideal. In doing so, it provides guidance for improving weak areas that are hindering growth or setting benchmarks for areas where over-performing might be the best course for developing or maintaining a unique position.

THE DEPENDENT VARIABLE

The vast majority of studies should include a dependent variable. The dependent variable is a question respondents answer that addresses their overall attitude toward a company, product, or service. Depending on the topic of your study, here are two questions you could use as dependent variables. The first question here relates to future purchase intention, while the second relates to general attitude:

In the future, how likely are you to buy [insert name of company/product/service]?
– Definitely will buy.
– Probably will buy.
– Might or might not buy.
– Probably will not buy.
– Definitely will not buy.

Overall, how would you rate [insert name of company/product/service]?
– Superior.
– Excellent.
– Good.
– Fair.
– Poor.

A dependent variable can also relate to other company or product goals. If you are striving to achieve a high-quality image or the best customer service, the dependent variable question could be:

When it comes to high quality, how would you rate [insert company/product/service]? A "10" rating would mean that you rate it the highest quality, a "1" rating would mean the lowest quality, or you could rate it anywhere between 10 and 1.

When it comes to customer service, how would you rate [insert company/service]? A "10" rating would mean you rate its customer service the highest, a "1" rating would mean you rate it the lowest, or you could rate it anywhere between 10 and 1.

Perhaps your dependent variable is frequency of purchase. For example:

Think about the next 10 times you purchase [insert product]. How many of those times would you purchase [insert product]?

The dependent variable is important in measuring what your overall market effort is trying to influence. If your goal is to get more people to buy, you want to understand the key factors that you should address to achieve greater purchase. If your goal is to convince people that you have the best customer service, you want to know the precise actions that will affect a stronger perception of your customer service.

There are several ways to use the dependent variable. Table 17.4 shows the attitudes of respondents toward several factors on the basis of their purchase intent. Notice how the data are split out by respondents indicating that they will likely purchase in the future compared to those who are unlikely to purchase.

By using the dependent variable in this manner, it is easy to see that those who are likely to purchase more strongly agree that the Bob catalog has great customer service and carries unique products. Those less likely to purchase agree strongly that the company has low prices but not great customer service.

Ultimately, the goal would be to convince the less likely to buy customer to become more likely to buy. From Table 17.4 it is reasonable to conclude that they would need strong convincing that the company has great customer service and unique products.

The same would be true when using other dependent variables. If people who think you have a great company or will give you a larger percentage of their purchases hold certain strong attitudes, you'd conclude that those are the attitudes you'd want everyone to hold.

Therefore, in determining your dependent variable, think about the action or opinion you are trying to achieve. Simply set up banner points that compare the positive attitudes you have achieved for some respondents to the negative attitudes you would like to change for the other respondents. Then you can look at the areas that have to be improved to

Table 17.4   Respondents' rating of the Bob catalog

Agree strongly the Bob catalog:	Respondents who said they would:	
	Definitely/probably purchase %	Probably not/definitely not purchase %
Carries unique products	50	20
Has easy ordering	20	25
Has low prices	30	50
Has great customer service	60	10

move the negative respondents into the same mindset as the positive respondents.

GOING BEYOND CROSS-TABS

Chapter 16 on statistical techniques discusses a number of techniques that you can use to provide additional insight into your data. Deciding whether to go beyond the cross-tabs is usually driven by the time you have to dig deeper into the data and your willingness to employ a statistician.

It's my experience that 90 percent of your learning will come from simple cross-tabs and t-tests. If, after digging through the tabs, you're still scratching your head, get to an experienced market research statistics person who speaks in "non-stat," if you know what I mean. I don't mean a pure statistician here. I mean a statistician experienced in survey research, one you can usually find by asking your tab supplier for a referral.

Market research statisticians can be magical in what they might do with your data and the new perspectives they can bring. Discuss what you think you've learned and why you're still struggling. Ask whether some regressions might clarify what's important or whether a TURF analysis could help you set clear priorities. I will guarantee you one thing – how surprised you'll be that a relatively small sum of money spent on stats can bring a fuzzy study to life and set you off on the best course of action.

ANALYTIC SATISFACTION

When should you be satisfied that you have pruned your study for all it's worth? Some analysts will spend very little time with data, and the story will come to them. They have a knack for quickly seeing where the results point and the actions that they should take. In such cases, "over and out."

Other analysts sweat the data. They have a personal curiosity and tenacity for digging beyond the obvious. They are naturally inquisitive and not content with the first answers that emerge. They like the challenge of turning seemingly insignificant data into creative findings. By taking their time to do so, they produce unique action plans that wouldn't otherwise have surfaced.

Analytic satisfaction depends on the scope of your study and your tolerance for complex stories. I would say this, though. The first few times that you analyze research data, review your conclusions with a research professional. The analytic learning curve is steep – so steep, in fact, that attempting to analyze anything but the simplest of research efforts by yourself would likely be unwise. Retaining a research professional during your initial analytic efforts is prudent. Without doing so, your best learning is likely to remain hidden in the data.

WRITING A REPORT

If you work for a company for which it is important to write a research report, your best bet, initially, is either to follow old reports that others have written or that you can dig up from other sources, or to bring in a research professional for a couple of hours of consultation on how to write a report.

Market research reports can be highly detailed or relatively simple summaries of the information. The nature of your study and the reasons for even writing a report are important in determining its scope. If you are a research supplier or work in the research department of a company, you would probably write a report that is detailed enough so that strangers could get a complete picture of the project. If you are writing for a small audience that you interact with frequently, going overboard on detail is probably unnecessary.

Whoever your audience, below is a general outline that is followed when writing a research report for a survey:

1. *Title page.* This is a simple title describing the study and the month and year it is being issued.
2. *Study objectives.* This is usually a bullet-point page that outlines the primary and secondary objectives of your study.
3. *Study methodology.* This is a description of how data were collected, the number of interviews that were conducted, a description of the target respondents, and where and when the study took place.
4. *Management summary.* A two- to four-page text description of the key findings will suffice for the management summary. Findings written in brief bullet points usually work best.
5. *Recommendations.* Recommendations should be apart from the management summary. The recommendations and actions that you as the report writer feel come from the data can be quite different from other perspectives. This section should put forth what you feel the data imply but in a tone that allows others to have different opinions.
6. *Detailed findings.* This section should consist of research tables that highlight the key data that emerged from the cross-tabs. The data can

be depicted on simple tables that you create or can be shown graphically. At the top of each table or chart should be a one- to three-sentence description of the points that the table makes.

7. *Demographics.* The demographics of respondents in the survey can be depicted in tables or charts and should appear toward the end of the report.

8. *Appendix.* The appendix consists of the questionnaire used for the study plus other documents that might be important for a better understanding of how the study was conducted.

In writing a focus group report, points 1 through 5 above can be followed. The writing of the detailed findings section (point 6 above) of a focus group report is somewhat like writing a book. It consists of a text discussion of what was learned in the study. Take the following sub-section titles from the actual detailed findings section of a focus group report:

- *Sub-section A.* Needs and wants for the ideal clothing catalog.
- *Sub-section B.* What distinguishes one catalog from another.
- *Sub-section C.* Attitudes toward catalog customer service.
- *Sub-section D.* Major areas where catalogs can improve:
  - Speed and efficiency of service.
  - Assortment and choice.
  - Personalization.
  - Having a caring attitude.
  - Price.
  - Providing information.

In each of the above sub-sections, up to five pages of text were written elaborating on the topic. Sometimes, actual quotes from respondents are used to make a point or illustrate an attitude. In all, the detailed findings section of a focus group report can be very short and to the point or a lengthy treatise on the attitudes, perceptions, and ideas that emerged.

There is no need to put a demographic section (point 7 above) in a focus group report, although the discussion guide and screeners should be part of the appendix.

18

Putting results into action

By now, you should have a good idea of the importance of marketing research. Hopefully you are clear on how to plan a study, execute it, and analyze the results. But I would say that, for many of you, the battle has just begun.

If you are the sole research action-taker, consider yourself lucky. You have no one to blame but yourself if the research isn't used to its fullest. But, if you have anyone else to convince of the virtues of your study, you are likely to face challenges.

There are many research reports that are tactical in nature in which results point to a clear course of action. There is little to communicate or mull over. You read the results, and the action steps jump from the page. You move ahead confident of the direction you're taking.

But there are many studies that are very strategic in nature or have course-changing implications. Such studies are usually open to interpretation and differing points of view. Alternative action steps might be costly or drain company resources that could be better used elsewhere.

Studies with far-reaching implications are usually a challenge to digest for all they are worth, and the status of the people charged with putting the data into action will play a pivotal role. All in all, then, it is wise to process meaty studies in a collaborative manner – where viewing the alternatives should be done from various viewpoints and where having team "buy-in" is important before moving ahead.

If you are the boss, people are likely to pay more attention when you communicate the results. And you can always choose to dictate the direction that you want to follow. But if you need the support of others, the task can be difficult.

Unequivocally, the worst thing you can do with your research report is to circulate it and hope that people will be moved to action.

Communicating research results can be categorized into two groups. First, if you want to waste your effort:

- Circulate the report and hope people get something out of it.
- Circulate the report and wait for feedback.
- Circulate the report with your recommendations for action and wait for action to happen.
- Do the above using only a short summary of the report.
- Do the above without setting dates for discussion or feedback.
- Let the report sit until you feel it's the right time to show it to others.

Second, if you want to optimize your effort:

- Consider the report as the beginning of a process to change course, take new actions, or examine new opportunities.
- Consider the report as a stimulus to brainstorming.
- Consider the report as a starting point for discussion of previous strategies and potential new ones.
- Consider the report as having companywide impact that, if used correctly, will benefit everyone.

In order to optimize the use of the research by you, by others in your company, or by outside consultants or vendors, try the actions detailed in the following sections.

Circulating the report with a subsequent presentation date

It is one thing to circulate a research report and quite another to motivate people to read it before a presentation. There is no doubt that, if the report is read or studied prior to being presented, it will amplify results.

Circulating a proposed action sheet

Attach a proposed five-point action sheet when you circulate the report. Check with everybody one day prior to the presentation to make sure their sheet is completed. If not, cancel the presentation.

The five-point action sheet should appear as follows:

1a. Research finding:

_____

1b. Action idea:

_____

2a. Research finding:

_____

2b. Action idea:

_____

3a. Research finding: ·

_____

3b. Action idea:

_____

4a. Research finding:

_____

4b. Action idea:

_____

5a. Research finding:

_____

5b. Action idea:

_____

Using the presentation to kick off action

If a research presentation ends with people nodding or agreeing that the results were "interesting," "surprising," "nothing really new," and so forth, you have just wasted your money. It is likely that nothing more will happen – at least, nothing of consequence.

Immediately following the presentation and with everyone present, go over their action suggestions. Write the ideas on an easel. Brainstorm new ideas as you go.

Have each person rank the action ideas and post the scores. Use a simple three-point rating system as follows:

1. Let's get started on that one.
2. Ideas with merit but in need of greater thought. Revisit in two weeks.
3. Longer-term good ideas. Revisit in three months.

Champion the process

As with everything worth accomplishing, a champion is critical. Someone must *own* the research and the process.

Completing the above steps is a great start but, if responsibility for action is in several hands, follow-through is also essential. It is usually productive for the person championing the research to stay with the process even after the research is complete.

The best-laid action plans will get bogged down unless someone is their champion. Further, the best action plans have a way of morphing into something that wasn't suggested by the research in the first place. At realistic intervals, the study champion should meet personally with the people assigned to take action on the various tasks. The relevant research findings and actions should be reviewed to determine whether they are still on target and moving forward.

Review the research three months later

It's worth the time for everyone to reconvene and view the same research presentation again, in retrospect. Review the actions that have been taken and the results. If all the meeting accomplishes is to reinforce that actions have been or are being taken, there will be satisfaction that the research has made an important contribution. But, importantly, time has a way of altering perspective.

Revisiting the results will suggest better approaches for implementing action that has not been taken. Time will also bring to light actions not previously conceptualized. Most importantly, it will prove again that research is a dynamic tool and an important part of the company and its momentum.

Periodically review the research

A study is always timely until a new study replaces it. Just because six months or a year passes doesn't mean that your study is irrelevant. When new company problems and challenges surface, revisit the research. You'll be amazed at the new insights that pop off the pages of old reports.

LAND MINES

Getting research utilized to its fullest not only requires a process, a champion, and follow-up, but it requires knowledge of land mines. Chief among those is the not-invented-here syndrome.

There will always be someone who is the group skeptic – the person who, for whatever reason, enjoys taking the role of devil's advocate. I can hear it now:

- "Why didn't you interview more people?"
- "Well, our customer service people tell us different."
- "Please explain again exactly how you conducted that regression analysis."

There are people who just don't want to acknowledge research as objective or unbiased and will be threatened or intimidated by the changes that might be indicated by your study. Status quo people will just kill research – if you let them.

Another land mine is "What you're suggesting will take too long a time." Well, that's total nonsense. If everything were an easy fix you'd already be doing it. If you conduct research in the first place you undoubtedly have problems to fix. You have an itch in your business that needs scratching. What a shame to go through the whole process only to be discouraged from changing because of the time you think it takes. Try keeping in mind that the rate of change is always magnified while you are doing it.

Then there is the response "We're already doing that." This land mine is the ultimate in protecting turf and resisting improvements. My thought to such a remark is "Doing what?" I will assure you that you might be doing something but it's not getting the emphasis that the research is suggesting. If the research itself is questioning what you're doing, you can be pretty sure that you could be doing it a lot better.

Yet another great land mine is the attitude of "What's in it for me?" This is often covert and not an easily discernible attitude. If the data are suggesting change and you have people justifying the status quo, you have a big problem. What is discouraging about this attitude is that you can conduct research until you're completely broke, and no amount of cajoling or even fear of being fired will motivate such self-centered employees to work on improving the situation. Maybe firing them is exactly what you should do!

TRY THE BONUS SYSTEM

In working for hundreds of companies, I've known only one that used research results to determine staff bonuses. The results the company received, particularly from its customer service people, were amazing. It never ceases to amaze me why companies are as resistant to tying the giving of bonuses to research as they are.

Research can be used as an incentive for improving almost any company function. Tracking studies that provide attitude measurements of company image, product satisfaction, incidence of purchase by new customers or repurchase by existing customers, money value of purchases, customer satisfaction, and many others are great motivators for your staff when a bonus is at stake.

Conduct a benchmark tracking study. Take measurements across the company functions that touch customers and prospects. Set up a company bonus pool that can be paid out partially or completely. Set tracking study levels that must be improved in order for bonuses to be paid.

Present the benchmark results to key company managers, tell them how much money is at stake for their departments, and give them the tracking study levels that must be achieved. Then, importantly, let them and their staffs have the autonomy to do as they see fit to improve the levels.

Conduct another study in three to six months and start paying the bonuses where they are deserved. You can also watch happily as the departments that don't achieve bonuses redouble their efforts during the next period – and as your company bottom line improves.

A FINAL WORD

Researching the marketplace never stops. Just by having an open mind, you will be bombarded in the media by new research, facts, and information that will help you grow your business. You don't even have to try that hard.

But you and your business will be better served if you do take a proactive approach. The internet is an ever-expanding sea of information. Use it often. Ask it questions about your business. Go to the library. Talk to friends and relatives. Do everything that is free and that your time allows.

But as your business grows, you will reach a level of sophistication where continued growth will be dependent on the answers only primary research can provide.

I hope that you are encouraged to budget money every year for marketing research. You'll find that it stimulates creativity and generates inspiration to explore new options. You will vastly improve the manner in which you think about your business and you will make smarter choices. Most importantly, you will make more money.

Glossary of terms

cost per interview (CPI)   The cost of a research study can be viewed in cost-per-interview terms. By taking the total cost of the research (e.g., $20,000) and dividing by the number of interviews (e.g., 200), the CPI is derived (e.g., $100). The CPI allows companies pricing research from competing suppliers to determine which supplier is providing the most competitive price. CPI comparisons should be viewed from various points of view (e.g., the services the supplier will provide, their experience and expertise, and their ability to provide research results when needed) in determining which supplier to use.

creative consumers   Respondents who tend to be more verbal, expressive, and able to speculate about issues and ideas. They are often more aggressive and opinionated about issues than non-creative consumers. They are particularly helpful when developing new ideas or products.

discussion guide   A dynamic outline listing the areas that a moderator would address in a qualitative study. Areas of questioning on a guide often change to better address issues that emerge during the discussion.

error range   In any type of research there is always statistical error around a number. This is the range around which the data could be expected to vary either higher or lower were the research to be reproduced or conducted repeatedly. The larger the sample of target respondents, the smaller the error range. Most marketing researchers consider +/−5 percent as an acceptable error range.

exploratory research   An umbrella term that indicates the research is limited in nature. It is often conducted when issues are unclear or when the marketer wants to keep up with market conditions and/or wants to better determine the need for larger-scale research.

field services Marketing research companies whose prime business is recruiting respondents for qualitative research or administering questionnaires for quantitative studies. Field services do not generally offer strong consultative services and are best used as data collection sources when a knowledgeable researcher provides clear direction to them.

focus groups Allow issues to be observed and ideas and theories generated. They can help in determining the research objectives that should be addressed in follow-up research efforts. Focus groups do not determine if an issue is true for one person or a million people. They (as well as any other type of qualitative research) should be used to do no more than surface the fact that an issue or idea exists.

full-service supplier Marketing research company that can conduct a research study from beginning to end, and is generally consultative in nature. Full-service suppliers are often looked to in helping determine research objectives, in questionnaire development, for collecting and tabulating data, for using any special statistical procedures when analyzing data, in preparing a report and recommendations on the findings, and for the presentation of results.

interviewer- and self-administered questionnaires Self-administered questionnaires are filled out by the respondent. Interviewer-administered questionnaires must employ an interviewer to ask the questions of the respondent. There are different considerations when constructing an interviewer-administered questionnaire as against one that is self-administered.

level of confidence The confidence that the researcher can have in getting the same answers from fresh-sample target respondents if the study were reproduced or conducted repeatedly.

overall research objective A one- or two-sentence statement that captures the essence of the learning that is expected from the research.

probing Following up on an answer that a respondent gives to a question to determine deeper, underlying attitudes. Probing is most common when conducting qualitative research. Often, though, survey questionnaires use open-ended probing techniques to understand better why respondents gave the answers that they did.

projectable research A research sample size that is large enough for the results to be indicative of how the target population in general would answer the same questions.

qualitative research An umbrella term for small-sample research that is not projectable. Non-projectable research is used to generate opinions and hypotheses about customer and prospect attitudes. It does not determine which opinions and attitudes are most important. It encompasses a variety of research techniques including focus groups, one-on-one interviews, and brainstorming sessions.

quantitative research   An umbrella term for large-sample survey research that is projectable. Results can be generalized to large-population targets. Telephone, internet, mail, and personal or mall intercept are the common interviewing techniques used when collecting quantitative data. Quantitative research is often used to validate findings discovered in qualitative research.

questionnaire   The script that is used when collecting data for a quantitative survey. Interviewers do not and should not vary from asking the questions exactly as written and in the order written. A questionnaire is not a dynamic tool.

research action plan   Broad term for the actions that the marketer might take before the research is conducted. It can also refer to the exact actions and timetable for implementation once the research results are available.

research control   For many research studies it is necessary to compare one set of data to another set of data, called the control. By viewing data from the control, it is possible to determine where the marketer is at a competitive advantage or disadvantage as against competitors. Also, when the marketer wants to change or improve its marketing efforts in whatever areas improvement might be needed, the control allows determination of whether the alternative approaches being considered are superior to the current approach and, therefore, should be adopted.

research objectives   Objectives that directly relate to clarifying the goals of a market research study. Research objectives are often derived from marketing objectives that have been previously agreed to. Clear research objectives are essential for determining the most action-oriented questions to ask when creating questionnaires or discussion guides.

research professional   Broad term for a person who has specific experience working in marketing research. The length of time a person has worked in the research industry coupled with expertise in a wide array of research techniques generally determines the level to which he or she can claim to be a professional researcher.

respondent   The person to whom questions are being asked.

specific research objectives   Sets out the important specific areas where information is needed to address effectively the overall research objective.

statistical significance   A mathematical procedure that determines whether two sets of data should be considered different from each other. It allows the researcher to conclude on whether the answers from one group of target respondents are different from those of another group. It allows determination as to whether certain marketing approaches are more appropriate for one target than for another.

statistical techniques   A broad number of mathematical procedures to which data are applied. They are used most often in more sophisticated research and can provide direction so that the researcher can do a better or more complete job when analyzing the data.

strategic research   A type of study that assists in determining the most promising and profitable courses of action. It provides basic information about the marketplace so that overarching brand or company marketing strategies can be determined.

tab plan   The plan that the researcher provides to a firm that specializes in tabulating and arraying answers from survey questionnaires. In creating a tab plan the researcher is compelled to determine how the data will be analyzed.

tabulations (tabs)   The raw data that emerge from tabulating and arraying the answers from survey questionnaires. It is from the tabs that the researcher will analyze the data, report findings, and make recommendations.

tactical research   Research that is limited in nature and that assists in determining how best to achieve the overarching strategic direction. It helps determine the important smaller elements that will be effective for achieving the overarching strategic direction.

target respondents   Respondents from a desirable segment of the population.

valid sample   A sample derived from a representative sampling procedure (the manner in which research data are collected). Having a valid sample means that the attitudes of the people interviewed can be assumed to be the same as the attitudes of the people not interviewed.

Index

Further reading

Levinson, Jay Conrad (1990) *Guerrilla Marketing Weapons: 100 Affordable Marketing Methods for Maximizing Profits from Your Small Business*, Plume Books, New York

Levinson, Jay Conrad (1998) *Guerrilla Marketing: Secrets for Making Big Profits from Your Small Business*, 3rd edn, Houghton Mifflin, Boston, MA

Levinson, Jay Conrad (2004) *Guerrilla Marketing for Free: Dozens of No-Cost Tactics to Promote Your Business and Energize Your Profits*, James Bennett Pty Ltd, Belrose, New South Wales

Levinson, Jay Conrad and Godin, Seth (1995) *The Guerrilla Marketing Handbook*, Houghton Mifflin, Boston, MA

Levinson, Jay Conrad and Lautenslager, Al (2005) *Guerrilla Marketing in 30 Days*, Entrepreneur Press, New York Levinson, Jay Conrad, Frishman, Rick, and Lublin, Jill (2002) *Guerrilla Publicity: Hundreds of Sure-Fire Tactics to Get Maximum Sales for Minimum Dollars*, Adams Media Corporation, Avon, MA

ALSO AVAILABLE FROM KOGAN PAGE

The *Market Research in Practice* series

Published in association with the MRS.

"An important initiative to provide a series of core texts, not only to support professional development for researchers, but also to enable marketing and general managers to become more aware of the applications and value of market research."
David Barr, Director General, MRS

"The new Market Research [books] are excellent... We are adopting them as core texts on our CIM research courses. They offer students... the opportunity to study market research topics separately and in depth."
Graham Webb, Senior Programmes Manager, Park Lane College

**Business to Business
Market Research**
Understanding and Measuring
Business Markets
Ruth McNeil
0 7494 4364 2   Paperback   2005

Consumer Insight
How to Use Data and Market Research
to Get Closer to Your Customer
*Merlin Stone, Alison Bond,
Bryan Foss*
0 7494 4292 1   Paperback   2004

**The Effective Use of
Market Research**
How to Drive and Focus Better
Business Decisions
Robin Birn
0 7494 4200 X   Paperback   2004

Market Intelligence
How and Why Organizations Use
Market Research
Martin Callingham
0 7494 4201 8   Paperback   2004

Market Research in Practice
A Guide to the Basics
*Paul Hague, Nick Hague,
Carol-Ann Morgan*
0 7494 4180 1   Paperback   2004

Questionnaire Design
How to Plan, Structure and Write Survey
Material for Effective Market Research
Ian Brace
0 7494 4181 X   Paperback   2004

**Researching Customer Satisfaction
and Loyalty**
How to Find Out What People
Really Think
Paul Szwarc
0 7494 4336 7   Paperback   2005

For full details, to download a sample chapter or to order, visit:

www.kogan-page.co.uk/marketresearch

ALSO AVAILABLE FROM KOGAN PAGE

"This really makes marketing happen – congratulations!"
Professor Malcolm McDonald

"All marketing lecturers find your book most useful – it is replacing Kotler on both the strategic and tactical parts of our courses."
Mats Engström, IHM Business School, Sweden

"Practical tips and a useful chapter on brand management."
Media Week

0 7494 4298 0   Paperback + CD ROM   2004

For further information on how to order, visit our website